# Elements of Style 2017

### Edited & Compiled by
### Richard De A'Morelli

SPECTRUM INK PUBLISHING
"Tomorrow's Great Authors and Classics Today"

## Elements of Style 2017

**ISBN numbers:**
978-1-988236-26-1 ~ mobi
978-1-988236-27-8 ~ epub
978-1-988236-28-5 ~ paperback
978-1-988236-31-5 ~ paperback (large print)

**Spectrum Ink Canada**
Vancouver, British Columbia

**Spectrum Ink USA**
San Luis Obispo, California

**Online:**
http://vu.org/books/

# What This Book Will Do for You

This book presents a comprehensive roundup of grammar, style, and punctuation rules for writers and others who must edit and proofread reports, term papers, and other documents. It is inspired by and loosely based on Strunk's *Elements of Style*, a classic published in 1918 and still widely used today. Strunk's book is brief, and some of the rules he discusses are out-of-date; but a more serious shortcoming is that technology and the rise of self-publishing have brought a deluge of new grammar and style rules writers and editors must learn. *Elements of Style 2017* greatly expands on Strunk's short guide and includes more than 250 pages of up-to-date grammar, style, and punctuation rules for modern writers, with easy-to-follow examples.

Concise writing is essential in today's competitive world. Your manuscripts and other documents must be free of grammar and punctuation errors. But you cannot self-edit your work unless you recognize these errors when you see them. The rules presented in this book will help you to identify these mistakes and will guide you through the creative process of writing, revising, self-editing, and proofreading.

This style guide may be useful to a wide range of readers in various settings:

• Writers of all skill levels will discover quick and pain-free ways to recognize and fix grammar, style, and punctuation errors in their manuscripts.

• Students can use these rules to improve the clarity and flow of term papers, book reports, essays, and other homework.

• Teachers can use this book to help students understand grammar, style, and punctuation rules without the tears.

• Employees can follow these style guidelines to produce well-written reports, manuals, brochures, and other materials in the workplace.

Good writing offers compelling rewards. If you are an author, a cleanly edited manuscript may bring an acceptance letter from an agent or publisher; or if you self-publish on Amazon, it could bring positive reviews and sales. For students, an impressed instructor could mean an A grade; and in the workplace, an impressed supervisor could mean a pay raise, a promotion, or a successful business venture.

Choose any chapter of this book, read and follow the straightforward advice, and you will see an overnight improvement in your writing. Read a chapter a day, and in a few weeks, you will be amazed by the polished quality of your final draft.

You can become an awesome writer. Learn how to improve your grammar and style, and take your writing to the next level!

# About the Author

Richard De A'Morelli published his first magazine feature article at age fourteen and signed a multi-book contract with a traditional publisher at eighteen. Since then, he has published 15 nonfiction books on writing and inspirational topics, three novels under pseudonyms, and more than 500 by-lined newspaper and magazine articles.

Richard has produced and taught online courses on creative and technical writing, Web design, Javascript programming, and motivational topics at Virtual University. He also taught journalism, writing, and self-help courses in traditional classrooms at Los Angeles Valley College and Learning Tree University in Southern California.

Beyond freelance writing, Richard has 30+ years of experience as a professional editor. He was a by-lined editorial staff member to the late bestselling author Irving Wallace, and he has held management-level editorial positions with numerous book and magazine publishers.

Richard resides on California's scenic Central Coast where he freelances full-time as a writer, editor, and software developer.

| | |
|---|---|
| Home | http://my.vu.org/writers/richard |
| Facebook Profile | http://facebook.com/writer2 |
| Facebook Page | http://facebook.com/jedi.editor |
| Google+ | http://google.com/+RichardDeamorelli |

## Other Spectrum Ink Books by the Author

- *You Can Change Your Life*
- *As a Man Thinks*

For details or to order, visit http://vu.org/books/

# Acknowledgments

The content in this book is comprised of the author's original material remixed with updated and revised content drawn from various sources including: *The Elements of Style* (William Strunk Jr.); *Practical Grammar and Composition* (Thomas Wood); *U.S. Government Printing Style Manual* (2008 ed.); *Punctuation: A Primer* (Frederick W. Hamilton); *How to Speak and Write Correctly* (Joseph Devlin); *Guide to the Marking Assignments* (Ian Johnston); and *Wikipedia*. Cover photo elements are licensed from Adobe Stock Photos.

This book makes frequent references to the *Chicago Manual of Style* (16th Edition) and *AP Stylebook* for writers of American English; and *Oxford Style Guide* for writers of British English. Examples of stylistic differences are given throughout the book. This volume is not intended as a substitute for any of these comprehensive style guides. It may be used as a learning tool and a quick-reference alternative, but if you are a publisher or editor, you should rely on the latest version of the style guide applicable to your projects.

## DEDICATION

This book is dedicated to my wife Barbara with love
and appreciation for putting up with my quirky personality
for the past twenty years.

# Table of Contents

# PART I

# GRAMMAR AND STYLE RULES

# Chapter 1
## Grammar and Style for the 21ˢᵗ Century

Years ago, when my first magazine article was published shortly after my fourteenth birthday and I set my heart on writing as my life's goal, there weren't many resources for aspiring writers. Amazon.com was decades off in the future. We purchased paperbacks from the local bookstore, subscribed to *Writer's Digest* magazine, and borrowed the paltry handful of books offered by the public library. I owned several dictionaries, a thesaurus, some paperbacks on writing and vocabulary, a high school grammar textbook, and a thin book with a cloth cover and faded pages: *The Elements of Style* by William Strunk Jr. It was an indispensable reference that I reached for often when writing and editing my early books and articles.

It has been nearly a century since Strunk's book was published. Today, it is a classic, used by many college students, writers, and even some editors as a quick reference. Some of the grammar rules outlined in the book are as true today as they were a century ago. But as the years have passed, one by one, these rules have become outdated. Another shortcoming is that many grammar and style rules which contemporary writers should follow today are missing from his book.

Last summer, I set out to update *Elements of Style*, intending to delete the obsolete rules and add some new ones. As I worked through the project, I thought: "Wait, maybe I should add this...and this...and this." As the weeks went by, my supposedly quick update exploded into 250 pages packed with updated grammar and style rules. So, while this present volume was inspired by and is loosely based on Prof. Strunk's grammar book, I have included a wealth of material from other sources, cited in the Acknowledgments, and I mixed in my own original material as well.

Most people in this age of technology and instant self-publishing are writers, although many don't view themselves in that light. Some are aspiring novelists, others are published authors or bloggers; and millions are writers by virtue of the fact that they are called upon to write content for work, school, or leisure activities. Many of these reluctant wordsmiths get a glazed look when English grammar rules come up in discussion. Just the mention of the words "grammar" and "style" confuse some, and few know the difference. Simply put, grammar is concerned with how words are used and put together to form sentences and paragraphs. Style refers to an additional set of rules some writers, and all professional editors, follow to edit and proofread book manuscripts and other documents. A knowledge of grammar is important because it will help you to write sentences that make sense. Style rules are just as important because they make it possible for you to turn a rough first draft into a final draft manuscript or a publication-ready document.

Style rules cover a wide range of issues, above and beyond basic grammar, from questions on word usage to capitalization, punctuation, how to abbreviate, and how to write numbers. Style rules fill in the gray areas that exist because some grammar rules tend to be broad. For example, *Chicago Manual of Style*, the world's most widely referenced style guide, advises that numbers up to one hundred must be spelled out, and values over that should be written as digits. Thus we would write: *The alphabet has twenty-six letters, and a year has 365 days.*

When we stray from consistent adherence to basic style rules, let's take a look at what can happen:

> Nine men stood by the wall, and 4 women stood next to the 2 cars. When the police approached the 9 men, they scattered, and the four women jumped into the two cars and sped away.

This hodgepodge of digits and spelled-out numbers makes the above paragraph seem badly written. Inconsistent style disrupts the flow of a manuscript, making it difficult for readers to follow. Diligently adhering to style rules from start to finish will result in a well-written manuscript that the writer can hand in at work or school, submit to an agent or publisher, or self-publish with a reasonable expectation of positive reviews and sales.

In online writing groups and at social gatherings, some writers can be heard arguing that grammar and style don't matter—it's the story that counts! In fact, that's not the case. Surveys have shown that book buyers expect published works to be cleanly edited and free of typos. Badly edited books—and unfortunately, many self-published books fall under that heading—typically see few or no sales and receive harsh reviews from readers who know good writing from bad and don't mind saying so.

Numerous style guides are used today. The most widely recognized are: *Chicago Manual of Style*, the bible of editors working in American English fiction genres, and some nonfiction editors; *AP Stylebook*, used by journalists and many others who write and edit for news organizations and websites; and *Manual of APA Style*, used mostly by college students for writing term papers and essays. In the United Kingdom, *Oxford Style Guide* is widely followed. Many other style guides are used in government, academia, and by niche publishers.

Modern style guides are packed with rules on grammar, punctuation, and related matters. A working editor might have devoted months or years to learning these rules. This investment of time and the level of skill required to do a good job at editing presents a high bar for writers who want to self-edit and submit a manuscript to a publisher with the imprimatur of being cleanly edited and proofread, and for those who wish to self-publish but cannot afford to hire an experienced editor.

One downside of style guides is that they sometimes offer conflicting advice, which can be confusing to writers and even editors. *Elements of Style* will tell you to write one way; *Chicago Manual of Style*, or CMoS, may tell you to do the opposite! As an example, CMoS mandates the use of serial commas, while *AP Stylebook* advises against them. So if you are editing to AP Style and use a serial comma, it's an error; if you follow Chicago Style and don't use a serial comma, that's an error. Many novice writers don't even know what a serial comma is, and since it is important for you to know, let's dive right in and start learning.

A serial comma is a comma placed before the coordinating conjunction in a list of three or more items. The first sentence below is punctuated with a serial comma after the word *oranges*; it is omitted in the second sentence.

Chicago Style:

She bought apples, oranges, and pears.

AP Style:

She bought apples, oranges and pears.

Similarly, Chicago Style and AP Style both require that the period at the end of a dialogue passage be placed inside the closing quotation mark. However, Oxford Style advises that the period should be placed outside the closing quote mark as in the second sentence below:

Chicago and AP Style:

Mary said, "Some of these rules are confusing."

Oxford Style:

Mary said, "Some of these rules are confusing".

## 1.01 | *Grammar and style made easy.*

The task of compiling a handbook on writing style that demystifies and simplifies the subject is challenging because the accuracy of the advice depends on, among other things, whether you are writing fiction or nonfiction, and even where you live in the world. Most writers just want to write, and few aspire to become editors or proofreaders. Consequently, I have kept this book as simple as possible. For the most part, I defer to grammar and style rules consistent with *Chicago Manual of Style*, with occasional references to *AP Stylebook*.

Ultimately, the goal of this book is to give writers of both fiction and nonfiction a reasonably pain-free way to self-edit, proofread, and polish their manuscripts without having to memorize a thousand pages of rules intended for professional editors. While there is no substitute for the skill of a competent editor or the eye of a skilled proofreader, if you take the time to learn and apply the rules discussed in these pages, you should be able to self-edit your writing and take pride in the manuscript you submit to an agent or publisher, or that you self-publish.

## 1.02 | Are these hard-and-fast rules?

Style rules are intended as guidelines to enforce consistency in writing, editing, and proofreading. Unlike grammar, which has specific rules that usually should not be broken, style rules are to some extent based on editor and publisher preferences (house rules), and industry standards, such as how and when to spell out numbers, and whether to use serial commas. The major style guides differ in fundamental ways, and no two editors will ever produce the same result, even if they follow the same rules, because editing inherently involves some degree of subjectivity. Nevertheless, following a set of style guidelines will enhance readability and give a writer's work the polished quality readers expect from a well-edited and carefully proofread manuscript.

## 1.03 | Write clearly.

Clear, concise writing is not a choice but a requirement in today's world. Readers have developed a habit of skimming content on the Web, and this behavior carries over into their digital and print book-reading habits. Few people have the time or patience to muddle through the convoluted prose found in much of the literature from the previous century. Modern writing styles call for shorter paragraphs and concise, crisply written sentences which are easy to read and understand.

Writing can be defined as: the art of communication using the science of grammar. The writer's objective is to inform and entertain readers by communicating facts or a story efficiently. The clearer your writing, the more likely it is that readers will grasp the meaning of your words and enjoy the information or stories you share.

## 1.04 | *Be consistent.*

Good writing is built on patterns, so whether you are writing a news story, a press release, a sci-fi novel, or a spicy love story, you must be consistent in your writing structure and style. Don't refer to an iPhone in one paragraph and call it a cell phone in the following paragraph, and a mobile device in the next. Likewise, avoid using different numbering schemes in which you write "*10 pens*" in one sentence and "*ten pens*" in the next. Readers will notice these variations, and they will be distracted trying to figure out your rationale for switching back and forth.

Be consistent with punctuation too. If you use serial commas on the first page of your manuscript, use them on the next page and on through to the end, ensuring that every sentence is consistently punctuated rather than handled in a hit-and-miss fashion.

## 1.05 | *Consider your audience.*

The best writers anticipate and answer readers' questions or entertain them with great stories. Identify your intended audience before you sit down to write. Think about what your readers already know and what they might want to know about your topic, or what they will expect from your story to enjoy it. Consider their level of reading comprehension, the depth of their interest, and what is the norm or common in your chosen genre. Avoid the attitude that you must "dumb down" your writing so that average people can read it. You readers are smarter than you might think! Focus on writing clearly and concisely so they can learn from the information you provide or enjoy the story you tell.

## 1.06 | *Write short paragraphs.*

Avoid long paragraphs. Large blocks of text are daunting and alert your reader that what is to come may be monotonous and difficult to read, or boring. Shorter paragraphs are more inviting and easier to understand. Try to limit paragraphs to four or five sentences, or about 100–125 words. A paragraph should discuss one main idea, not several. It is possible an idea will require twenty sentences to properly develop, but that doesn't mean you should have a twenty-sentence paragraph that runs an entire page. Look for logical places where you can break a lengthy block of text into several paragraphs.

In a long paragraph, you will probably have at least a few transitional terms. For example, you may have started a sentence with a word or a phrase such as *Next, Furthermore, In addition,* or *However.* You can break a paragraph at this point and allow the next paragraph to begin with one of these transitions. Just make sure that the resulting smaller paragraphs are unified in themselves.

## 1.07 | **Write concise sentences.**

For the same reason that lengthy paragraphs should be avoided, you should aim to write crisp, concise sentences that are easy to read and follow. In past decades, complex syntax with lots of word clutter was in vogue; today, readers find the classics of yesteryear verbose and hard to follow. Modern readers process information more readily when it is presented in small chunks; longer sentences require more effort to figure out. In the two examples below, the first is wordy; the second is succinct. You can probably guess which of these passages most readers would prefer:

✗ In light of the fact that the report does not include specific examples in its discussion of ways to improve workplace safety, we are of the strong belief that it should undergo revision.

☺ We believe the report should be revised because it does not include examples of how to improve workplace safety.

## 1.08 | **Three points of view for writing.**

In your writing, you can use three points of view: first person, second person, and third person. Each point of view expresses a different relationship to the reader.

*First person* is when the person is speaking. Stories written from this point of view make use of first-person forms of personal pronouns (*I, we, me, us, my, our, mine,* and *ours*). This voice is used in memoirs and similar works. It is sometimes used in fiction writing; but telling stories in this voice is challenging and requires considerable skill. Most writers don't handle first-person point of view especially well.

> **I** spent the summer touring the scenic mountains of Oregon and Washington. **My brother and I** shared the driving, and **we** camped out under the stars.

*Second person* represents a person or thing spoken to. This voice is sometimes used in nonfiction writing, especially in the self-help, how-to, and do-it-yourself genres. It is rarely used in fiction. Second-person pronouns include *you, your,* and *yours.*

> For a summer adventure, **you** can tour the scenic mountains of Oregon and Washington. If **you** travel with a companion, **you** can share the driving and save money by camping out under the stars.

*Third person* is when the character, event, or object is spoken about. This is the voice most often used for writing news and other nonfiction, and for most fiction. Third-person pronouns include: *he, him, his, she, her, hers, they, them, their, theirs, it,* and *its.*

> Charles spent the summer touring the scenic mountains of Oregon and Washington. **He** shared the driving with **his brother** and camped out under the stars.

## 1.09 | Choosing the appropriate voice.

The point of view appropriate for a project will depend upon what you are writing and your target audience. Once you have settled on a point of view, stay with it and don't shift from one voice to another. If you decide to write in third person, maintain that point of view throughout your manuscript.

The short paragraph below is written in second person (you). This voice can be confusing for readers and difficult to follow when the word *you* is used as a general pronoun. In the example, the writer's statement that "you can generate electricity in several ways" is awkward, and it's not relevant to readers who aren't involved in a utility business that produces steam for power-generating turbines.

Most commercially available electricity is generated by turbines that convert steam into electricity. **You can produce steam in several ways.**

With a few quick edits, the voice can be easily changed to third person:

Most commercially available electricity is generated by turbines that convert steam into electricity. **Steam can be produced in several ways.**

Notice that changing the voice improves the flow, and removing the general pronoun "you" gives the passage a more authoritative tone.

# Chapter 2
## Unlock the Magic of Your Words

Despite the ease of self-publishing, the book industry today is quite challenging. Competition is intense. In 2017, an estimated 500,000 new books will be published on Amazon. A small number will be marketed by traditional publishers and micro-publishers, or "indies"; many will be self-published. A comparative handful of these self-published titles will be well written and professionally edited, but most won't. Unedited books typically sell less than a few dozen copies over their lifetime; so the prospects of financial success are slim. Hiring an editor costs money, and most self-published writers cannot invest hundreds or thousands of dollars on editing services which they are unlikely to recoup.

The goal of this book is to provide a set of easy-to-follow grammar and style rules that writers of all skill levels, from beginner to veteran, can use to self-edit and proofread their own documents for work or school, as well as articles, short stories and book manuscripts. Whether you plan to submit your work to a publisher or agent, or you've decided to self-publish, you should find these guidelines and tips useful. If you only read one section of this book and apply what you learn, your writing will be noticeably improved. Well-edited content free of glaring grammar errors and typos will please your readers, and satisfied readers will be more apt to post positive reviews and help you advance toward your goal of creative and financial success as a writer.

So our starting premise now is that everyone is a real writer! But there is a difference between writing words and producing a polished, final draft; a difference between jotting down thoughts and telling a story, painting a picture, provoking emotion, moving readers to laugh or cry, think, or react to the issues of our day. Everyone with a pen or keyboard can write, but truly good writers are uncommon. Read on and learn how you can join the ranks of great writers who write truly awesome books.

## 2.01 | Great writing is a skill you can learn.

The ability to weave words into a tapestry of expression like delicate threads in fine linen, and to write in a way that informs and entertains, is a skill. In some people, it's a natural talent; others become competent writers through hard work and perseverance. Yet, even those who are born with writing talent must learn the fine points of grammar and style to write sparkling prose. No one sits down and becomes a master storyteller on the first try. It's a learning process. In these pages, you will be given a road map to help you master useful tips and tricks of the craft. Follow this map and you will be able to achieve every wordsmith's fondest goal of being an accomplished writer whose words may change the world or touch the lives of everyday people.

Whether you aspire to write a novel, a technical handbook, a short story, a love letter, or a gripe to a local newspaper, the rules are the same: you must think before you write, say what you mean, get to the point, and express it well. Readers today have a limited attention span. Everyone is in a hurry, bores quickly, and has virtually unlimited reading material to choose from; much of it is free. Thus, you should not write a 500-word paragraph describing a cloudy sky or flowers in a garden when you can describe that scene in a single, concise sentence.

There is no infallible recipe for success as a writer, but a few ingredients are essential: you need a knowledge of grammar and style; an interesting story to tell; basic writing talent; and a willingness to write, rewrite, and polish, moving a rough draft to a final draft. Throw in a dash of wit and a pinch of creativity, and you are on your way to crisp, captivating prose.

## 2.02 | Think clearly, write creatively.

Clear thinking is another important ingredient that even experienced writers sometimes lack. Know what you want to say before you sit down and start writing. This is obvious advice, certainly, but it's a stumbling block for many writers who proclaim, "I just want to write!" Lacking a definite story plot or goal, they write before they think and fall into a sea of wordiness and confusion. A builder must have a blueprint and must know each step required to erect a structure before pouring the foundation. Likewise, writers must have a message, a destination, and a blueprint or road map of how to move their stories from start to finish before they embark on the creative journey.

If you have ever stalled on a particular paragraph or at a certain point in your story, and you found yourself struggling, writing and rewriting, chances are it is because you have lost track of your story or what you want to say. When you think clearly, you will write clearly, and your words will shine. When your thoughts are muddled, your writing will be muddled, and you will struggle to get your thoughts into words.

For the thirty years that I have taught writing classes, both in physical classrooms and online, I have lectured on this point many times: "Know what you want to say before you sit down to write." Many other writers and writing instructors offer the same advice. In *A Creative Approach to Writing*, Roger Garrison observes:

"All writing is in a real sense creative. No matter what form the writing takes, the writer must solve certain problems which are the same whether he is doing a paragraph theme of simple exposition or a publishable short story. He must know what he is talking about, be able to think it through, organize it reasonably and persuasively, and present it with clarity, attractiveness, and vigor. Surely, in a fundamental sense, this is a creative process.

"This is another way of saying that good writing begins with good thinking. Most teachers of writing know this. They recognize with renewed force each year that nearly all their students' writing problems are basically thinking problems. The muddled phrasing, mixed-up sentences, and badly constructed paragraphs of typical freshman themes, for example, are obvious demonstrations of the confused thought processes that produced them."

Knowledge is power, and your words are a conduit for that power. Writing can provide the keys to unlock doors to wonderful things in life.

Developing your talent can help you secure a better job, better pay, and other trappings of success, which are hard to come by in today's economically challenging times. Cultivating your writing talent can have benefits on a personal level too. It can endow you with the power to express your feelings and ideas, and the confidence to do so. It can brighten your life outlook, deepen your sensitivity, stimulate your imagination, even take you into the realm of nirvana. Whatever doors might be opened by this talent, one thing is certain: Learning to write, and polishing your skill so that you become a better writer, will change your life.

## 2.03 | Energize your writing style.

If you are writing for your own enjoyment, editing your work is not of paramount importance. But if you are writing for others, then your goal is to communicate with your readers and do it well. You need a message or a story that will resonate with your audience—a set of facts, breaking news, an idea, a gripping horror tale, a love story. You'll want to write with impact, turning dry facts and words into informative and entertaining reading. If you approach this right, even a boring technical manual can be presented in a way that is interesting and fun to read.

The following sentence is dry and merely states a fact:

> Tomorrow will be hot and smoggy with highs in the nineties.

Precise writing of this sort is appropriate in some situations. But more often, even if you are writing a technical manual, you will have the latitude to present details in a more interesting way. Readers want to be informed, but they don't want to be put to sleep with a monotonous recitation of facts. Help the reader "see and feel" your words, not merely look at them on a page. This is why fiction has been popular since the dawn of language and remains so today—it lets readers live vicariously through the eyes and minds of your characters, or through your own eyes if you are writing news or other nonfiction. Even news factoids can give readers a "you-are-there" sense of what is being reported. The trick is for you to put the effort into writing the story in a compelling way.

Words can open a window to sights, sounds, and worlds beyond your reader's humdrum life. But going too far the other way to spice up drab prose can be just as problematic.

> Tomorrow will be sizzling hot and terribly smoggy, with scorching highs blasting into the blistering nineties.

Wordiness may fill the pages of a book quicker, but it will put off most readers, making them yawn and giving them a reason to find something else to read. Avoid verbosity, or wordiness. Also, avoid flowery writing that borders on the absurd. Find the middle ground; this is where your readers will be looking for you. Aim for a writing style that is fresh—one that brings your words to life, makes your story interesting, and leaves your reader thinking, "This is a great story, and it's well written too!"

## 2.04 | What a difference a word can make!

How you cobble words into sentences, and sentences into paragraphs will shape the quality of what you write and how readers react. By changing just one word in a sentence, you can alter the mood and paint a slightly different picture—or a remarkably different scene—in your reader's mind. One well-chosen word can set the mood, even if you are writing a factual article. Therefore, put thought into your words and choose carefully, especially during revisions and as you self-edit your project.

Consider these short sentences. We will change one word, the verb, and discover what a difference a word can make, creating a different mood.

> The girl **ran** down the hallway.

> The girl **skipped** down the hallway.

> The girl **danced** down the hallway.

> The girl **staggered** down the hallway.

Now let's inject another word into the sentence: *frightened*, an adjective. Again, we can see that a slight tweak can make a difference in what your reader perceives. The first sentence below illustrates this point; the second sentence shows how matching the right adjective and noun can create suspense. The third shows how an incorrect word choice can throw things off—it makes no sense that a frightened girl would dance down the hallway, so this sentence leaves readers wondering whether the writer has made a careless mistake or needs a dictionary.

The **frightened** girl **ran** down the hallway.

The **frightened** girl **staggered** down the hallway.

The **frightened** girl **danced** down the hallway.

As you revise your manuscript and self-edit, tweaking your words to perfection, choose carefully. Try to make every word count. Avoid word choices that make no sense, called "absurdities" in grammatical terms. Take care that you don't write contradictory prose such as, "The boiling water was cool to the touch," or "He shouted softly." A few careless word choices can turn a writing into one that leaves readers laughing, and the writer is the butt of the joke.

## 2.05 | What do you want to say today?

Verbosity, or excessive wordiness, is like giving your reader a suitcase full of bricks to haul—you are asking her to carry the extra weight, but there's no reward for doing so. Using more words doesn't mean that you are making a clearer point or telling a more interesting story. Often, the opposite is true. Verbosity can bog down your reader in confusing and unnecessary word clutter.

The next time you sit down to write, ask yourself: "What are the main points I want my reader to know from reading this story or this part of the story?" Note your answer. If you are unable to sum it up in a few short sentences, you haven't thought out your project well enough that you are ready to proceed. After writing down the focus, make a short list of secondary points that relate to the main theme. Then, use this thumbnail sketch to develop a rough outline of your story. With this synopsis, you are ready to begin writing! You can follow this quick and easy process to create a road map for any new writing project or idea.

Remember:

**Unclear thoughts produce unclear writing.**

To achieve the best possible result in the shortest amount of time and with the least amount of effort in your writing, you must know where you are going before you begin the trip. When you embark on your literary adventure with a road map, you'll be able to create a well-organized series of sentences that you can build into smooth-flowing paragraphs, which in turn will flow into a well-written story.

## 2.06 | Redundancy: many words, no substance.

Redundancy is another common pitfall that can befuddle even veteran writers. Restating the same point in several ways, mentioning facts that are obvious to most readers, and using several words together that mean nearly the same thing, can bog down a story in tedious detail and obscure your message. For example:

> Mary hurriedly squeezed a glob of toothpaste from the plastic tube of toothpaste on the bristles of her toothbrush, opened her mouth, and proceeded to quickly brush her teeth.

Your reader knows where toothpaste comes from and how to use it. Pare down this clumsy sentence and omit the words that state the obvious. If Mary is squeezing a tube of toothpaste, we can assume she's holding it in her hand; and most toothpaste containers are plastic. If she hurriedly squeezed the tube, it restates the obvious to say that she brushed quickly. We know, too, that a toothbrush has bristles, and we don't need to be told that Mary opened her mouth to begin brushing. When we strip all the word clutter away, we see that only a few words in the sentence are relevant:

> Mary squeezed a glob of Colgate onto her toothbrush and quickly brushed her teeth.

Better yet:

> Mary quickly brushed her teeth.

Or throw in a few "action" details to make the scene flow better and give the reader a sense that the story is going somewhere:

Late for work, Mary quickly brushed her teeth and dashed out the door.

Writing complex and meandering prose doesn't make for an interesting story. Relevant details, presented in an interesting way that the reader will enjoy, provides the secret sauce of an interesting book or article.

## 2.07 | Before and after: The art of rewriting.

Rewriting is a necessary step in the creative process that any writer who wishes to produce polished prose must do. Rewriting begins with a rough draft and allows you to shape it into something better. Look for sentences you can rephrase to improve the clarity or flow of your story. Look for better ways to get the important points across. Make sure those points are brought into focus and not lost in a jumble of words.

Rewriting is not the final polish that gives a manuscript its luster, but a step in the process. It brings you closer to a near-final draft, where you can make last-minute tweaks, such as replacing a particular word with a better choice, correcting or smoothing out grammar, fine-tuning your style, and making other minor improvements. Then, you wrap up the project with careful spell checking and proofreading.

## 2.08 | Writing prompt—Imagine the possibilities!

If you ask a dozen writers to write a paragraph on the same topic, you will get a dozen wildly different results. A word or phrase, an idea, or a bit of imagery such as a setting sun or the squeak of a door will conjure unique scenes in each writer's mind. As an optional writing exercise, consider the short excerpts from four literary classics presented on the next page. Choose two passages from each classic (for a total of eight) and work them into a story of your own creation. Write about 1,000 words—it can be a short story, the opening chapter of a novel, or whatever you like. Select your passages carefully and put some thought into how you can work them into a story. Practice what we have discussed: Make every word count and trim word clutter. Put some thought into this writing challenge and you may end up with an interesting story you will want to develop further!

Excerpts from *Walden Pond:*

He was only a little more weather-beaten than when I saw him last.

"We are so degraded that we cannot speak."

It is darker in the woods than most suppose.

We easily come to doubt if they exist. We soon forget them.

Excerpts from *The Secret Garden:*

At that very moment such a loud sound of wailing broke out...

"I suppose you might as well be told something–to prepare you.

You are going to a queer place."

On and on they drove through the darkness, and though the rain stopped, the wind whistled by and made strange sounds.

Excerpts from *The Red Badge of Courage:*

Finally, he said: "You don't know everything in the world, do you?"

He turned to shout over his shoulder, "Don't forget that box of cigars!"

The men stumbled along still muttering speculations.

He lay down in the grass. The moon had been lighted and was hung in a treetop.

Excerpts from *The Wizard of Oz:*

It really was no miracle. What happened was just this...

Just as he spoke there came from the forest a terrible roar.

On and on they walked, and it seemed that the great carpet of deadly flowers that surrounded them would never end.

Then a low, quiet voice came, and these were the words it spoke:

## 2.09 | Metaphors, similes, and clichés.

A *simile* is a comparison between two generally unconnected things, and the comparison is typically drawn using the words *like* or *as*.

Bob eats **like** a horse.

Sally was **as mad as** a hornet.

Ed has been **as busy as** a bee.

That idea went over *like* a lead balloon.

A *metaphor*, like a simile, is a figure of speech, but it is based on some resemblance of a literal to an implied subject:

William has **a heart of gold**.

The wind was **a gentle murmur in the leaves**.

Maria drowned **in a sea of grief**.

The accounting report was **fishy**.

When metaphors and similes turn up on social media or elsewhere, writers may pick them up and reuse them. Soon, the expressions become popular and are heard everywhere. But even the most popular metaphors fall out of favor. When that happens, they become clichés.

A *cliché* is a stale metaphor or other well-worn expression that has lost popularity. The English language is littered with abandoned metaphors. Lazy writers may continue using clichés, which tips off readers that a story is dated or the writer needs to catch up with the times.

A good rule of thumb for avoiding clichés in your writing is that if you have heard a popular metaphor, millions of others have heard it too. If you use it in your writing, by the time others read your work, the phrase likely will be a cliché. Therefore, avoid recycling metaphors borrowed from others, and put some thought into creating your own metaphors!

## 2.10 | Show don't tell...what does that mean?

The importance of clear, concise writing has been stressed, but that doesn't mean your prose should be sterile. *She was angry!* is concise but bland, and it doesn't draw readers into the scene. Many people visualize the words they read on a page. Your readers might imagine events you have described and hear characters speaking dialogue in your story.

A hallmark of great writing is that a story must show rather than tell. You do this by writing a scene in such a way that it plays out in the reader's mind as it would if he were watching a video. It is possible to do this whether you are writing a grisly horror story, a touching love story, or a technical manual. In *The No-Experience-Necessary Writer's Course*, Scott Edelstein observes: "A successful story or poem—or for that matter a successful line, sentence, stanza, or paragraph—shows the reader what is happening rather than merely tells him or her about it."

Edelstein compares two sentences: *Jenny was angry!* and *Jenny bit her lip and slammed the book shut!* He explains: "The first sentence is devoid of sensory information and merely states how Jenny feels. The second reveals Jenny's feeling through two specific sensory details: the sight of her biting her lip–and sound–of her slamming the book closed. These images enable us to actually see her anger and, more importantly, feel it...Nowhere in the second sentence does the word 'anger' appear. We don't need to be told that Jenny is angry because the sentence shows us her anger. Biting her lip also implies that she's trying to hold some of her anger back."

Inexperienced writers are often confused by the "show don't tell" directive. After all, writing is all about telling a story or communicating facts. Writing *Jenny was angry!* is telling. Showing means revealing Jenny's anger through her actions—biting her lip, slamming the book; perhaps her eyes flashed or her cheeks flushed red. You are still telling details of the story, but you are doing it in a way that shows, allowing readers to see and hear those details.

# Chapter 3
## Choosing Words, Building Sentences

### 3.01 | *Use everyday words.*

Clarity is everything in writing, and concise writing depends upon your choice of words. When you describe an elevator as "a vertical transportation unit" or you refer to a leaky pipe as a "plumbing rupture," clarity goes out the window, and so does your reader's attention span and interest. For fiction, you can write colorful prose but still use everyday language to tell a story your readers can easily understand and enjoy. For nonfiction, communicate relevant facts in the clearest and most direct way possible without sacrificing interest.

An emphasis on clarity doesn't mean you should limit yourself to three-letter words; but use familiar, everyday words as much as possible. Avoid using obscure words most readers won't recognize. If you have to look up a word in the dictionary, it's safe to assume many of your readers will need to look it up too. Most won't bother, so you may lose a large segment of your audience before they turn the page.

You can add clarity to your prose by avoiding stilted and unnecessary phrasing, known in some writing circles as "gobbledygook." Instead, use concrete words familiar to most readers and that have clear meanings. Whenever possible, replace words in the table below with the suggested alternatives or similar words.

| ✗ Gobbledygook | ☺ Suggested Alternative |
| --- | --- |
| accordingly | so |
| accrue | add, gain |

| | |
|---|---|
| additionally | also |
| advantageous | helpful |
| adversely impact | hurt, harm |
| ascertain | find out, learn |
| caveat | warning |
| commence | begin, start |
| consequently | so |
| consolidate | join, merge |
| constitutes | is, makes up |
| demonstrate | prove, show |
| disseminate | give, send |
| enumerate | count |
| equitable | fair |
| expeditious | fast, quick |
| facilitate | ease, help |
| feasible | possible |
| forfeit | give up, lose |
| furthermore | also |
| heretofore | until now |
| herewith | here |
| inasmuch as | since |
| incentivize | encourage |
| methodology | method |
| moreover | also |
| necessitate | cause, require |
| notwithstanding | in spite of |
| obligate | require |
| preclude | prevent |

| | |
|---|---|
| prioritize | rank |
| proficiency | skill, ability |
| promulgate | issue, publish |
| remuneration | payment |
| render | give, make |
| subsequently | after, later, then |
| terminate | end, stop |
| therefore | so |
| utilize | use |
| validate | confirm, verify |
| whereas | because, since |
| wherefore | why |
| whereupon | just after; and then |

## 3.02 | Write with a word, not with a phrase.

With the previous rule in mind, take your editing a step further and trim phrases comprised of multiple words when a single word works just as well and makes your sentence clearer and easier to read.

**✗ As a matter of fact**, I'm having second thoughts at this point in time.

☺ **In fact**, I'm having second thoughts now.

**✗ During the period** I was in Mexico, there is no doubt but that I had a great time.

☺ **While** I was in Mexico, I had a great time.

When you find any of the awkward phrases in the table below in your writing, replace them with the suggested alternatives or similar words.

| ✗ Try to avoid | ☺ Suggested alternative |
| --- | --- |
| a number of | some |
| a sufficient number of | enough |
| adjacent to | next to |
| as a matter of fact | in fact |
| at the present time | now, presently |
| at this point in time | now |
| by means of | by, with |
| close proximity | near |
| comply with | follow, obey |
| due to the fact that | since, because |
| during the period | during, when |
| for a period of | for |
| has a requirement for | needs |
| he is a man who | he |
| in a hasty manner | hastily |
| in a timely manner | on time, promptly |
| in addition | also, besides, too |
| in an effort to | to |
| in lieu of | instead of |
| in order that | for, so |
| in order to | to |
| in regard to | about, concerning |
| in relation to | about, with |
| in the amount of | for |
| in the event of | if |
| in the near future | shortly, soon |
| in the vicinity of | near |

| | |
|---|---|
| in view of | since |
| in view of the above | so |
| incumbent upon | must |
| is able to | can |
| is applicable to | applies to |
| is authorized to | may |
| it is clear that | clearly |
| not later than | by |
| on the ground that | because |
| pertaining to | about, of, on |
| prior to | before |
| provided that | if |
| pursuant to | by, following, per, under |
| relative to | about, on |
| set forth in | in |
| subsequent to | after |
| the question as to whether | whether |
| there is no doubt but that | no doubt |
| this is a subject which | this subject |
| until such time as | until |
| with reference to | about, regarding |
| with the exception of | except for |

## 3.03 | *Remove unnecessary words.*

Replacing overly formal phrases like ones above with one-word alternatives will add clarity and impact to your writing, but that's just the first step. You may be able to trim more word clutter from your sentences. Some writers provide more detail than is needed in a sentence; others use superfluous words, or fluff, that leads to dense, wordy construction. This is a common problem in both fiction and nonfiction writing. Long sentences full of words that serve no definite purpose are confusing and frustrating for readers. To illustrate that point, which of these two paragraphs do you think a reader would prefer?

> This letter concerns your request for records under the Freedom of Information Act. We received your request on August 10, 2016. We sent it to the Agency for Regulatory Policy. Unfortunately, the Agency cannot process your request without more information. We need you to reasonably describe the records you are seeking. Specifically, we need to know what records you need. Please advise us accordingly at your convenience.

Or this:

> We received your request for records under the Freedom of Information Act on August 10, 2016. Unfortunately, we cannot respond to your request until we know specifically what records you need. Please let us know at your convenience.

To remove word clutter from your sentences, become a tougher critic of your own writing. A sentence should contain no unnecessary words, and a paragraph no unnecessary sentences, just as a drawing should have no unnecessary lines. This doesn't mean that every sentence you write must be short; but every word in the sentence must play a role and either show or tell. Read each sentence carefully and look for unnecessary words you can trim without changing the meaning.

## 3.04 | *Don't double up terms.*

Some writers have a habit of placing two words with the same or very similar meanings in tandem, or next to one another, within a sentence. These "double terms" are redundant and add word clutter. If you notice a duplicated term in your writing and you can delete the word without changing the meaning of the sentence, then you should remove it.

    ✗ This fruit must be **washed** and **cleaned**.

    ☑ *Washed* and *cleaned* mean the same; use one or the other.

✗ The deeds must be **entered** and **recorded.**

☑ *Entered* and *recorded* mean the same; use one or the other.

✗ The program will **begin** and **commence**...

☺ The program will **start**...

**The measure and breadth** of the problem...

☺ **The scope** of the problem...

## 3.05 | Keep related words together.

The position of the words in a sentence is the main way that you show their relationship. So you should bring together the words related in thought whenever possible. For instance, the subject of a sentence and the principal verb usually should not be separated by a phrase or clause that can be moved to the beginning. However, this rule may be ignored when the interruption is deliberate as a way to create suspense.

In these below, the interposed phrase or clause interrupts the natural flow of the main clause. The noun is in **bold**; the verb is <u>underlined</u>.

✗ **Stephen King**, in his 1986 novel It, <u>reunites</u> seven adults who battled an evil creature when they were teens.

☺ In his 1986 horror novel *It*, **Stephen King** <u>reunites</u> seven adults who battled an evil creature when they were teens.

✗ **Corn**, when converted to alcohol, <u>becomes</u> ethanol and can be used as automobile fuel.

☺ When converted to alcohol, **corn** <u>becomes</u> ethanol and can be used as automobile fuel.

## 3.06 | Place modifiers next to the word modified.

Modifiers should be placed next to the word they modify whenever possible. If several expressions modify the same word, they should be written so that no ambiguity or incorrect relationship is suggested.

✗ **All the teachers** were **not** present.

☺ **Not all the teachers** were present.

✗ While walking in the park, Connie found a **silver** woman's **wedding ring**.

☺ While walking in the park, Connie found a woman's **silver wedding ring**.

✗ He **only** found **two typos** in the book.

☺ He found **only two typos** in the book.

In the next example, several clauses have been rearranged as suggested by this rule, with a noticeable improvement to the flow of the sentence.

✗ Jack Jones will give a lecture on Tuesday evening, to which the public is invited, on "The American Economy" at 8 p.m.

☺ On Tuesday evening at 8 p.m., Jack Jones will give a lecture on "The American Economy." The public is invited.

## 3.07 | Place long conditions after the main clause.

For the sake of clarity, long or wordy conditions (such as *if you own more than fifty acres and cultivate grapes* in the example below) should be placed after the main clause. In this way, you focus the reader's attention on the major idea you are conveying in the sentence, and then you explain the condition.

✗ **If you own more than fifty acres and cultivate grapes**, you are subject to water rationing.

☺ You are subject to water rationing **if you own more than 50 acres and cultivate grapes**.

## 3.08 | Avoid intruding words.

"Intruders" are another type of word clutter and contribute nothing to the meaning of a sentence. Common intruders include the words *program, event, effort, method, conditions,* and *activities*. In the examples below, the intruders are shown in **bold**. Notice that removing these words does not change the meaning of the sentences; in fact, doing so improves the flow.

✗ Library books and paper records are endangered by fluctuating temperature **conditions**.

☺ Library books and paper records are endangered by fluctuating temperatures.

✗ The new policy simplifies reporting **activities**.

☺ The new policy simplifies reporting.

✗ The declassification **effort** is proceeding on schedule.

☺ The declassification is proceeding on schedule.

## 3.09 | *Use contractions when appropriate.*

Contractions are shortened words made by combining several words and an apostrophe, such as *I'm*, *don't*, and *haven't*. Most people use them often in casual writing and speech. In the past, contractions were discouraged by grammar teachers as a sign of sloppy syntax. This is no longer the case. Today, writers are expected to adopt a friendlier, more casual tone. Contractions should be avoided in legal and technical writing as a rule; but in other writing, including fiction and general nonfiction, they may be used in moderation if the flow of a sentence would be improved. In addition, most English speakers rely heavily on contractions in verbal speech, so these expressions can be used liberally in dialogue to mimic natural conversation.

✗ We will make our best effort to provide the information you have requested.

☺ We'll do our best to provide the information you need.

✗ It is the hope of everyone at the Central Coast Wineries that our guests found the tour informative and enjoyable.

☺ We hope you've enjoyed our tour of Central Coast Wineries.

Apply common sense in using contractions. They should not be relied upon to such an extent that readers notice an over-abundance of them, except in dialogue, where failure to use contractions may give readers a sense that your characters' speech is stilted or too formal.

## 3.10 | Avoid redundancy.

*Redundancy* refers to the use of unnecessary words that repeat the same thought within a sentence. In most cases, redundant words and phrases are unnecessary and merely add word clutter. This is a common problem among writers, and it can give their prose an unpolished or amateurish quality. Some redundant expressions are funny; others are downright silly. But the bottom line is, they add no value to your sentences and bog down readers in tedious repetition.

You've probably heard the advice from a writing instructor or fellow wordsmith, "Avoid redundancy!" But what exactly does this mean? Let's consider some examples.

January is a month, so there's no need to write "the month of January." If the glass is full, it's full—saying it is "totally full" is redundant. A "hot water heater" is a redundant expression because the appliance does not heat hot water, it makes cool water hot—so it's simply a water heater. The word "destroyed" implies that something has been obliterated, so "completely destroyed" is repetitive and the adverb should be deleted. Use a modifier here only if you want to convey something significant or unexpected to the reader. For instance, you might write:

> The building was partially destroyed by the hurricane.

But it would be better to provide specific details and give your reader a sharper mental image:

> The building was damaged by the hurricane; the east wing was destroyed, but the two-story wing on the west was spared, except a few picture windows were blown out.

## 3.11 | **How to spot redundancy.**

Redundancy can take several forms: the chief offenders are *pleonasms* and *tautologies*. The former is a construction in which more words than needed are used to express an idea. The latter refers to a series of words used in parallel or close to one another that have the same meaning. The two are similar and often confused. For our purposes, it is sufficient to understand that both create word clutter and neither belong in a well-edited manuscript. Except in rare instances when a word or phrase is deliberately repeated by the writer for the sake of drama, redundant expressions should be deleted whenever you encounter them in your writing.

In these next examples, the repetitive words are italicized, and each sentence is followed by an explanation of why the wording is redundant.

> Her love story is **completely devoid** of emotion.
>
> Devoid means completely lacking so *completely* is redundant. This sentence is saying that her love story is *completely completely lacking of emotion.*

> I asked you to **repeat** that **again**.
>
> Repeat means "say again," so this sentence says: *I asked you to again say that again.*

> She was frightened and **shouted out loud**.
>
> Shouting is always loud and out loud, so *out loud* is redundant.

> The store **gave away free** samples.
>
> When samples are given away, *free* is redundant.

> I **know that** you are sad.
>
> In this sentence, the word *that* is redundant. If you want to use *that* for a bit of drama, you could write: *You are sad...I know that.*

I feel ill **at the present time**.

☑ *At the present* means "at this time," so *time* is redundant.

I am **absolutely certain**.

☑ Being certain implies belief is 100%, so it is already absolute.

## 3.12 | Redundant expressions to avoid.

The following list includes redundant expressions commonly found in writing that should be avoided.

| ✗ Redundant expression | ☺ Replace with |
| --- | --- |
| 12 o'clock midnight | midnight |
| 12 o'clock noon | noon |
| 6 p.m. in the evening | 6 p.m. |
| 8 p.m. at night | 8 p.m. |
| 9 a.m. in the morning | 9 a.m. |
| absolutely essential | essential |
| absolutely necessary | necessary |
| AC current | AC |
| actual facts | facts |
| advance planning | planning |
| advance warning | warning |
| affirmative yes | yes |
| all together | together |
| ancient fossil | fossil |
| and etc. | etc. |
| anonymous stranger | stranger |
| are now currently | currently |
| armed gunman | gunman |
| ascend up | ascend |

| | |
|---|---|
| attach together | attach |
| autobiography of my life | autobiography |
| awkward predicament | predicament |
| basic fundamentals | fundamentals |
| blood hemorrhage | hemorrhage |
| boat marina | marina |
| burning fire | fire |
| cash money | cash |
| circulated around | circulated |
| classic tradition | tradition |
| climb up | climb |
| close proximity | proximity |
| close scrutiny | scrutiny |
| cold frost | frost |
| cold ice | ice |
| collaborate together | collaborate |
| combined together | combined |
| commuting back and forth | commuting |
| completely annihilated | annihilated |
| completely blind | blind |
| completely deaf | deaf |
| completely destroyed | destroyed |
| completely empty | empty |
| completely expired | expired |
| completely filled | filled |
| completely full | full |
| completely ignored | ignored |
| completely thorough | thorough |

| | |
|---|---|
| completely unanimous | unanimous |
| connect together | connect |
| conniption fit | conniption, or fit |
| consensus of opinion | consensus |
| constant nagging | nagging |
| continuing on | continuing |
| DC current | DC |
| dead corpse | corpse |
| death threats on his life | death threats |
| definite decision | decision |
| depreciate in value | depreciate |
| descend down | descend |
| diametrically opposed | opposed |
| difficult dilemma | dilemma |
| drop down | drop |
| dry desert | desert |
| eliminate altogether | eliminate |
| end result | result |
| essential necessity | necessity |
| established tradition | tradition |
| exact replica | replica |
| exact same | same |
| exactly the same | the same |
| extra added features | added features |
| extreme hazard | hazard |
| familiar fixture | fixture |
| fellow colleague | colleague |
| filled to capacity | filled |

| | |
|---|---|
| final end | end |
| final showdown | showdown |
| first and foremost | first, or foremost |
| first conceived | conceived |
| forced compulsion | compulsion |
| foreign imports | imports |
| former ex-husband | ex-husband |
| former ex-wife | ex-wife |
| frank candor | candor |
| free gift | gift |
| freezing cold | freezing |
| frozen ice | ice |
| frozen tundra | tundra |
| full satisfaction | satisfaction |
| future ahead looks bright | future looks bright |
| future forecast | forecast |
| general consensus | consensus |
| genuine original | original |
| global pandemic | pandemic |
| good benefit | benefit |
| grand total | total |
| grateful thanks | thanks, appreciation |
| green in color | green |
| growing greater | growing |
| hear with one's own ears | hear |
| HIV virus | HIV |
| hot fire | fire |
| hot water heater | water heater |

| | |
|---|---|
| huddle together | huddle |
| imminent at any moment | imminent |
| individual person | person, or individual |
| indulgent patience | patience |
| inquisitive busybody | busybody |
| integrated together | integrated |
| intentional planning | planning |
| invited guests | guests |
| join together | join |
| joint collaboration | collaboration |
| joint cooperation | cooperation |
| killed dead | killed |
| knowledgeable experts | experts |
| lifeless corpse | corpse |
| linger behind | linger |
| literate readers | readers |
| live witness | witness |
| major breakthrough | breakthrough |
| major milestone | milestone |
| malignant cancer | cancer |
| manually by hand | manually |
| many frequent | frequent |
| marital spouse | spouse |
| married husband | husband |
| married wife | wife |
| may possibly | may |
| meandering around | meandering |
| mental thought | thought |

| | |
|---|---|
| merge together | merge |
| mesa table | table |
| missing gaps | gaps |
| month of June | June |
| more easier | easier |
| more than unique | unique |
| mutual cooperation | cooperation |
| my personal opinion | opinion |
| natural instinct | instinct |
| near proximity | proximity |
| necessary essentials | essentials |
| negative misfortune | misfortune |
| negative no | no |
| never, ever | never |
| new discovery | discovery |
| new innovation | innovation |
| new recruit | recruit |
| old adage | adage |
| old custom | custom |
| old senior citizens | senior citizens |
| only unique | unique |
| original founder | founder |
| original source | source |
| outside in the yard | in the yard |
| over and over again | over and over |
| overused cliché | cliché |
| pair of twins | twins |
| past experience | experience |

| | |
|---|---|
| past history | history |
| past nostalgia | nostalgia |
| past tradition | tradition |
| PC computer | PC |
| persistent obsession | obsession |
| personal friend | friend |
| please RSVP | RSVP |
| poisonous venom | venom |
| polar opposites | opposites |
| postponed until later | postponed |
| predict in advance | predict |
| previously listed above | listed above |
| quickly mushroomed | mushroomed |
| quite unique | unique |
| rags and tatters | rags, or tatters |
| real actual | actual |
| reason why | reason, or why |
| receded back | receded |
| refer back | refer |
| regular custom | custom |
| regular routine | routine |
| repeat again | repeat |
| resulting effects | effects |
| retreating back | retreating |
| return back | return |
| revert back | revert |
| rice paddy | paddy |
| rise up | rise |

| | |
|---|---|
| root cause | cause |
| round circle | circle |
| round wheel | wheel |
| ruling junta | junta |
| safe sanctuary | sanctuary |
| see with one's own eyes | see |
| seedling plant | seedling |
| serious danger | danger |
| sharp point | point |
| sink down | sink |
| small cubbyhole | cubbyhole |
| specific example | example |
| State of Nevada | Nevada |
| string together | string |
| successful achievement | achievement |
| sudden impulse | impulse |
| suddenly exploded | exploded |
| sufficiently enough | enough |
| sum total | total |
| surrounded on all sides | surrounded |
| the reason is because | because |
| tiny speck | speck |
| top priority | priority |
| total destruction | destruction |
| totally blind | blind |
| totally deaf | deaf |
| totally demolished | demolished |
| totally empty | empty |

| | |
|---|---|
| totally full | full |
| totally unnecessary | unnecessary |
| true fact | fact |
| tuna fish | tuna |
| uncertain indecision | indecision |
| undergraduate student | undergraduate |
| unexpected surprise | surprise |
| unhealthy sickness | sickness |
| unmarried bachelor | bachelor |
| unmarried old maid | old maid |
| unsolved mystery | mystery |
| useless and unnecessary | useless |
| usual custom | custom |
| vacillating back and forth | vacillating |
| very unique | unique |
| violent explosion | explosion |
| visible to one's own eyes | visible |
| water hydrant | hydrant |
| wet water | water |
| whether or not | whether |
| worldwide pandemic | pandemic |

# Chapter 4
## Grammar Rules Have Changed

**M**uch has changed in the realm of writing, editing, and grammar since the days that you sat in a schoolroom fighting to stay awake as your English teacher pretended to be excited discussing the parts of speech and scribbling conjugated verbs on the blackboard. Chances are, many basic rules were drilled into your memory, such as never start a sentence with the word *But;* never split an infinitive; and never end a sentence with a preposition. You might have followed these rules throughout life. But the world has changed, and the rules of English grammar have changed too. In this chapter, we will explore some of the grammar and style rules you were taught never to break that you can— and should— break in your writing today!

### 4.01 | Yes, you can split infinitives.

One style rule debated by writers in Facebook groups and elsewhere is whether split infinities are acceptable. An infinitive is a verb form that almost always begins with the word "to" and ends with a simple verb: to walk, to speak, to ask. A split infinitive is a short phrase in which a word, typically an adverb, in inserted between the "to" and the verb. For example: *to boldly go.*

Many believe there's a hard rule that infinitives never should be split. In fact, for the past two hundred years, English grammarians cautioned against splitting infinitives. The rule was adopted in the 1800s based on the notion that English derives from Latin, and it is not possible to split the infinitive of a verb in Latin because it is all one word. Present-day grammarians acknowledge that English isn't Latin, and the rule against split infinitives is now obsolete. *Chicago Manual of Style* advises:

"Sometimes it is perfectly appropriate to split an infinitive verb with an adverb to add emphasis or to produce a natural sound." That means you can now write a phrase like the venerable *Star Trek* line: "To boldly go where no man has gone before."

## 4.02 | **Ending a sentence with a preposition is OK.**

Another topic of debate in online writing groups is the premise that a sentence must not end with a preposition. This rule, like the obsolete rule on split infinitives, goes back decades, and it has changed too. According to Chicago Style: "The traditional caveat of yesteryear against ending sentences with prepositions is, for most writers, an unnecessary and pedantic restriction...The 'rule' prohibiting terminal prepositions was an ill-founded superstition."

In practice, some sentences may read better if the trailing preposition is eliminated. Sometimes the preposition it isn't even needed. Consider the following, where the first sentence ends with the preposition *at*, and the second sentence reads better without it.

> Where are you at?

> Where are you?

In English, a *phrasal verb* is a verb that consists of several words, and one word is always a preposition. Examples of phrasal verbs include: *cheer up, drop out, log on*. It is always acceptable to end a sentence with a phrasal verb. In these examples, the phrasal verbs are italicized:

> ☺ I hope you ***cheer up.***

> ☺ I love college, but I may have to ***drop out***.

> ☺ Before you can read your email, you must ***log on***.

A good rule of thumb to follow is that some sentences read better when rewritten to eliminate the preposition at the end. But there's no hard and fast rule against it, and you should not rewrite a sentence to awkward-sounding syntax just to remove a trailing preposition.

For convenient reference, a list of single-word prepositions is provided here, and a second list of multi-word prepositions follows.

## Single-word prepositions

| | | | |
|---|---|---|---|
| aboard | about | above | abreast |
| abroad | across | after | against |
| along | alongside | amid | amidst |
| among | amongst | around | as |
| astride | at | atop | before |
| behind | below | beneath | beside |
| besides | between | beyond | but |
| by | despite | down | during |
| except | for | from | in |
| inside | into | like | near |
| of | off | on | onto |
| opposite | out | outside | over |
| past | per | since | than |
| through | throughout | to | toward |
| towards | under | underneath | unlike |
| until | up | upon | via |
| with | within | without | |

## Multi-word prepositions

| | | |
|---|---|---|
| according to | adjacent to | ahead of |
| along with | apart from | as far as |
| as for | as of | as per |
| as regards | as well as | aside from |
| back to | because of | close to |
| due to | except for | far from |

| in addition to | in case of | in front of |
|---|---|---|
| inside of | instead of | left of |
| near to | next to | on account of |
| on behalf of | on top of | opposite of |
| opposite to | out from | out of |
| outside of | owing to | prior to |
| pursuant to | rather than | regardless of |
| right of | subsequent to | such as |
| thanks to | up to | |

## 4.03 | You can start a sentence with *And, But,* or *So.*

Another point of contention in writing groups and elsewhere is the question, "Can I start a sentence with a coordinating conjunction, such as *and, but,* or *so*?" This is one more grammar rule that was widely taught years ago, but it is no longer followed in modern style. Most writing style guides affirm that a sentence can be started with a coordinating conjunction, as long as the technique is not overused.

The Chicago Style Q&A forum on the Web offers this helpful advice: "*CMOS* includes Bryan Garner's opinion that there is 'no historical or grammatical foundation' for considering sentences that begin with a conjunction such as *and, but,* or *so* to be in error...The conjunctions *or* and *nor* can be added to the list. None of this means that it is not possible to abuse the privilege. Sentences should begin with a conjunction only when the result is clear and more effective than some other alternative."

Starting too many sentences with coordinating conjunctions can make your writing seem choppy and stilted. Even dialogue, which is more forgiving, can be monotonous if so many sentences begin with coordinating conjunctions that readers take notice. Therefore, use this sentence construction sparingly.

## 4.04 | Avoid the false subjects *it is, there is/are,* etc.

*False subjects* are phrases such as: *it is, it was, it will be, there is, there are, there was, there were,* and *there will be.* They usually occur at the beginning of a sentence and often displace the real subject. This is a lazy habit most often committed by novice writers, and it can cause ambiguity and awkward syntax. Avoid writing sentences with false subjects. In nearly every instance, a sentence that starts with a false subject can be rewritten to achieve an improved and grammatically correct result.

| Avoid false subjects: | Replace with: |
|---|---|
| It is revealed in the video | The video reveals |
| It was claimed by the prosecutor | The prosecutor claimed |
| There are times when | Sometimes (or Occasionally) |
| It will be announced by the candidate | The candidate will announce |
| There were failures because of | Failures were caused by |
| There will be protests unless | Protests will occur unless |
| It is her opinion that there are issues that need to be resolved. | She believes that several issues need to be resolved. |

## 4.05 | Minimize the use of *not.*

The word *not* is overused by many writers. It is clearer and more concise to say what something is or does than to say what it is not or does not do. Make definite assertions in your writing. Readers want to know what is going on; they're not interested in what is not happening. Avoid weak, non-committal prose.

| Avoid "not" constructions: | Replace with: |
|---|---|
| did not remember | Forgot |
| not on time | late |
| not honest | Dishonest |
| does not consider | Ignores |

| not precise | Imprecise |
|---|---|
| did not have much confidence in | Distrusted |
| He was not very often on time. | He usually came late. |
| He did not think that studying Latin was much use. | He thought studying Latin was pointless. |

While use of the word *not* for evasion should be avoided, it is acceptable to use as a means of denial or in antithesis. The antithesis of negative and positive is strong:

**Not** charity, but simple justice.

**Not** that I loved Caesar less, but Rome the more.

Be aware that negative words other than *not* (such as never, nobody, nothing, neither, and none) are usually strong and convey a sense of definite commitment to the reader:

The sun **never** sets upon the British flag.

The wounded man **never** gave up hope that he would be rescued.

The old woman called for help, but **nobody** came to her rescue.

**Nobody** believes that ridiculous claim from the candidate.

## 4.06 | *Which* and *that* are not interchangeable.

*Which* is not a more elegant or clever way to say *that*. The two words are not interchangeable, and the choice is not a matter of style—this rule is a right-or-wrong choice.

*Which* is a pronoun that introduces nonessential information. Use a comma before a *which* clause. If a comma won't work, then you should be using *that*. If you were to delete the words in the *which* clause, the remaining words should still form a full sentence.

*That* is a pronoun used to introduce essential information. Do not use a comma before *that*.

✗ Power plants **which** burn fossil fuels emit pollutants.

☺ Power plants **that** burn fossil fuels emit pollutants.

**✗** Power plants **that** are one source of electric power may emit pollutants.

☺ Power plants, **which** are one source of electric power, may emit pollutants.

To summarize: If you can use the word *that*, use it. If you don't have a comma before the word *which*, use *that*. If you delete the words in the *which* clause and the sentence does not make sense, use *that*.

### 4.07 | *He* and *I, you* and *me, myself.*

In English grammar, the words *I* and *me* are tricky and often confusing. One way to ascertain if you are using them correctly is to break the original sentence into two shorter sentences. If the wording of both sentences sounds correct when they are separated, you have written it correctly. If the wording sounds off, you are using *me* or *I* incorrectly.

☺ Give it to **him** and **me**.

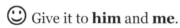 *Two sentences:* Give it to **him**. Give it to **me**.

**✗** Give it to **he** and **I**.

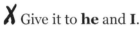 *Two sentences:* Give it to **he**. Give it to **I**.

This grammar question becomes more confusing when **he** *and* **I** are the subject of the sentence rather than the direct object.

☺ **He** and **I** went to the party.

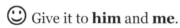 **Yes: He** went to the party. **I** went to the party.

**✗ Him** and **me** went to the party.

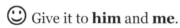 **No: Him** went to the party. **Me** went to the party.

☺ The party was fun for Sam and **me**.

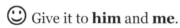 **Yes:** The party was fun for Sam. The party was fun for **me**.

The next three sentences use *me;* all are written correctly.

> Send the information to Mike and **me**.

> Send the information to **me** and Mike.

> Send the information to **me**.

When we break the next two sentences into separate clauses, we see that *Send the information to I* isn't correct, and asking someone to *Send the information to myself* doesn't work either.

> ✗ Send the information to Mike and **I**.

> ✗ Send the information to Mike and **myself**.

Here are a few more examples using *me, myself,* and *I*.

> ✗ The work was done by Christine and **myself.**

> ☺ I did the work **myself**.

> ☺ The work was done by Christine and **me**.

> ☺ Christine and **I** did the work.

## 4.08 | *None is/are, either...or, neither...nor*

Deciding whether an indefinite pronoun, such as *neither, none, no one, everyone,* and *some,* takes a singular or plural verb can be tricky.

When an indefinite pronoun is the subject of a verb, it is usually singular.

> ☺ **None** of the proposals was accepted.

> ☑ Although *None of the proposals* seems to require a plural verb, what we are really saying is: *Not one* was accepted. So, we must use a singular verb.

The following three sentences are written correctly:

> **Neither** answer was sufficient.

**Everyone** is happy today.

**Some** of the employees *are* in the lunch room.

When comparing two items, you must write *either...or* or *neither...nor*.

☺ **Neither** Robert **nor** I was planning to attend the wedding.

☺ **Either** Joyce **or** my boss was the last person to leave.

## 4.09 | A person is a *who*, not a *that.*

Use *who* with the pronouns *he, she, people,* etc. Use *that* with objects.

☺ He is the person **who** came to the meeting.

☑ He is the person **that** came to the meeting.

☑ (Many writers make this mistake.)

☺ This is the couch **that** I just bought.

✗ This is the couch **who** I just bought.

☑ (No one makes this mistake.)

## 4.10 | *Fewer, less, lower,* and *under.*

*Fewer* and *less* mean the same thing, but you use them in different circumstances. Use *fewer* for count nouns (things you can count) and *less* for mass nouns (things you can't count individually). Use *lower* for levels or percentages, and use *under* to describe location or spatial position (under the table).

Mass nouns:

less salt, less tired, less money, more work, less time

☑ Note that you cannot make mass nouns plural.

Count nouns:

fewer apples, fewer refiners, fewer dollars, fewer hours

Describing levels or amounts:

lower imports, higher prices, lower production (but watch for subtle nuances):

If the price of imports goes down, then write:

✗ fewer imports

☺ lower imports

If the quantity of imported items goes down, then instead write:

✗ lower imports

☺ fewer imports

✗ Gasoline costs under $4 per gallon.

☺ Gasoline costs less than $4 per gallon.

## 4.11 | Using "a" and "an."

The articles *a* and *an* have specific rules for usage, but knowing which article is the right choice can be tricky. For instance, should you write *a herb* or *an herb*? A refresher on a few basic grammar rules will help you sort things out and make the right decisions for flawless syntax.

Use *a* before singular, countable nouns that begin with a consonant sound, as well as letters and numbers that begin with a consonant sound, even if the first letter of the noun is a vowel.

She is **a** nurse.

He applied for **a** job.

I planted **a** tree in my yard.

I have **a** "1" in my street address.

She has **a** "U" in her first name.

He has **a** history of migraine headaches.

In the last three examples above, the number "1" is pronounced "won"; the letter "U" is pronounced "you"; and the first syllable of "history" is pronounced "his." All three consonant sounds take *a* in these sentences.

Use *an* before singular, countable nouns that begin with a vowel sound, as well as letters and numbers that begin with a vowel sound, even if the first letter of the noun is a consonant.

He is **an** engineer.

She saw **an** igloo in the distance.

I moved to **an** island paradise.

George has **an** "O" in his first name.

George also has **a** "G" in his first name.

We have **an** "8" in our phone number.

He had to wait **an** hour.

In the last three examples above, the letter "O" is pronounced "owe"; the number "8" is pronounced "ate"; the word "hour" is pronounced "au-er." All are vowel sounds, so the article *an* is used in these sentences.

Some words are trickier because pronunciation can vary by country and region. In American English, the *h* in *herb* typically is silent, so many Americans say "an herb." In British English, the *h* is often pronounced, so many Brits say "a herb." In some dialects in the U.K., the *h* in *hospital* is silent, so it's "an hospital" instead of "a hospital."

When *a* or *an* refers to an adverb or adjective written before a singular, countable noun, consider the initial sound of the adjective or adverb and follow the rules above to decide which article to use.

She is *an* **e**xcellent piano player.

Donald is *a* **r**eally unpleasant fellow.

Also remember: *a* and *an* can only be used with a singular noun. These articles cannot be used with plurals.

✗ She bought **an apples** at the grocery store.

☺ She bought **an apple** at the grocery store.

☺ She bought apples at the grocery store.

✗ The actress has **a dreams** of stardom.

☺ The actress has **a dream** of stardom.

☺ The actress **has dreams** of stardom.

Note that *a* and *an* are not used with uncountable and abstract nouns, which have no quantity. For example, *happiness, information, truth, air, advice, knowledge,* and *fun.*

✗ Joseph is in search of **a knowledge**.

☺ Joseph is in search of knowledge.

✗ Bob needs **a money** to retire.

☺ Bob needs money to retire.

✗ She asked the doctor for **an advice**.

☺ She asked the doctor for advice.

## 4.12 | *Must, May, Should, Shall and Will*

Avoid the ambiguous *shall.* The word can suggest either an obligation or simply a future event and the reader is left wondering. Whether you are writing fiction or nonfiction, it is never a good thing to expect your reader to second-guess or figure out what you mean.

• For obligation, use *must*:

You **must** pay your bills on time to avoid late fees.

The candidate **must** appeal to voters to win the election.

- For permission or to indicate possibility, use *may*.

  You **may** wear jeans to work.

  Jason **may** be late for work tomorrow.

- When suggesting an action or what ought to happen, use *should*:

  You **should** mow the lawn monthly to maintain a tidy front yard.

  To learn grammar and style, I **should** read this book carefully.

- When indicating something that is in the future, use *will*.

  My sister **will** spend July vacationing in Europe.

  I **will** pay my phone bill as soon as I deposit my paycheck.

## 4.13 | Use *first, second, third.*

Use *first, second, third* for connected points in text. Avoid the terms firstly, secondly, thirdly. These adverbial forms are widely perceived as stuffy and antiquated. If you have more than three points, consider numbering the items or using bullets.

## 4.14 | This is because... and that is the result of...

Do not begin sentences with *This is because, That is because, That is a result of, It is due to,* or similar phrases. These references are ambiguous and confusing. Repeat the subject from the previous sentence, even if it requires more words to complete the sentence.

  ✗ **This is because** of the new law.

  ☺ **This higher fee is because** of the new law.

  ✗ **It is due** *to* the weather.

  ☺ **The increase in demand is a result of** the weather.

## 4.15 | Often, *that* can be omitted.

Using the word *that* is often not necessary. While it is not wrong to include the extra word in most cases, modern style advises omitting *that* when you can do so without affecting the clarity of the sentence.

> **OK:** The lunch **that** I ate yesterday was good.

> **Preferred:** The lunch I ate yesterday was good.

> **OK:** The cars **that** were sold in 2015 have better brakes.

> **Preferred:** The cars sold in 2015 have better brakes.

As a rule, include *that* after verbs that imply assertion or speaking, such as: advise, advocate, agree, assert, assume, calculate, conceive, claim, content, declare, estimate, hold, imagine, insist, learn, maintain, make clear, point out, propose, state, and suggest.

> I assume **that** you passed your English test.

> He couldn't imagine **that** his wife would be unfaithful.

> Joe insists **that** he knows everything.

Include *that* before clauses beginning with conjunctions such as *after, although, since,* and *so.*

## 4.16 | Using *and, as well as, in addition.*

The words you write after *as well as* or *in addition to* are not as important as the words you write after *and.* Using *and* gives the noun or adjective that precedes and follows the conjunction equal importance.

> Prices went up because of weather **and** generator outages.

In the above sentence, the word *and* tells us that the weather and generator outages contributed equally to price increases.

> Prices went up because of weather **as well as** generator outages.

The phrase *as well as* implies a secondary importance, so generator outages are less of a factor in prices going up than the weather. The phrase *in addition* to has the same secondary importance.

## 4.17 | Avoid using *the fact that.*

Avoid phrases with the words *the fact that* to prevent word clutter. In most cases, *because* or a similar word can be used in place of phrases such as *In view of the fact that*, *Given the fact that*, and *In consideration of the fact that*. Replacing these stodgy and verbose expressions makes the resulting sentences shorter and easier to read.

**✗ In consideration of the fact that** college graduates earn higher wages during their working years, everyone should aspire to earn a four-year degree.

☺ **Because** college graduates earn higher wages during their working years, everyone should aspire to earn a four-year degree.

**✗ *Given the fact that*** you were promoted, your pay will go up.

☺ **Because** you were promoted, your pay will go up.

Other similarly wordy expressions can be replaced by shorter and more concise phrases as shown in the following table.

| ✗ Wordy expressions | ☺ Instead use |
| --- | --- |
| Allowing to the fact that | Since, or Because |
| In spite of the fact that | Though, or Although |
| Call your attention to the fact that | Remind you, or Notify you |
| I was unaware of the fact that | I was unaware (did not know) |
| The fact that he had not succeeded | His failure |
| The fact that I had arrived | My arrival |

## 4.18 | Avoid using *who is* and *which is/was.*

The words *who is*, *which is*, *which was*, and other similar expressions are often superfluous and usually can be eliminated without noticeable effect on your prose.

**✗** His father, **who is** an employee of the firm, has a law degree.

☺ His father, an employee of the firm, has a law degree.

✗ March, **which is** the third month of the year, has thirty-one days.

☺ March, the third month of the year, has thirty-one days.

# Chapter 5
## Action Words and Active Voice

### 5.01 | Don't hide the verb.

Verbs are called "action words" for good reason—they show action. They tell what happened or tell the reader what to do. Verbs are the heart and soul of clear writing and compelling prose. Choosing the right verbs can make a story or article more interesting and enjoyable to read.

Avoid turning verbs into nouns. Verbs turned into nouns are hidden and less effective. Hidden verbs require you to use more words than necessary, which leads to word clutter. Using strong verbs in place of noun phrases will make your writing clearer. Words to watch for that indicate a verb has been turned into a noun include the various tenses of: *do, give, have, make, perform, provide,* and *conduct.*

| Passive Verb | Active Verb |
| --- | --- |
| They did a study of | They studied |
| This gives the indication that | This indicates |
| This has the tendency to | This tends |
| We made the decision to | We decided |
| He provided an explanation | He explained |
| She conducted a review of | She reviewed |
| They gave a donation of cash and clothing... | They donated cash and clothing... |

## 5.02 | **Maintain consistent verb tenses.**

Maintain consistent verb tenses to clearly establish the timing of the action. Using one tense consistently and not switching back and forth will allow you to bring your reader into the story and connect the dots between one thought, scene, or event and another in a concise manner.

Inconsistent tense:

Natural gas **was created** by the underground decomposition of organic matter. Much of the carbon and hydrogen **is converted** to methane, the major component of natural gas.

The shift in verb tense from past (*was created*) to present (*is converted*) is confusing to the reader. It implies that the decomposition of organic matter happened in the past, but the conversion to methane is occurring only now. Writing the sentence correctly so that the verb tenses remain consistent eliminates this ambiguity.

Consistent tense:

Natural gas **is created** by the underground decomposition of organic matter. Much of the carbon and hydrogen **is converted** to methane, the major component of natural gas.

Do not change verb tenses unless you want to indicate a clear shift in time. For instance, the following is an appropriate shift in verb tense:

The policies **were** *adopted* in 2015. The policies **will be** *reviewed* in 2020.

The first sentence uses the past tense (*were adopted*) to indicate action that has already happened. The second sentence uses future tense (*will be reviewed*) to indicate action yet to come. This transition makes sense to the reader. Be careful that you write time transitions in a logical order and that they make sense.

## 5.03 | **Participial phrase agreement.**

A participle is a word formed from a verb and used as an adjective or a noun. A present participle typically ends with the suffix *-ing,* and a past participle often but not always ends in *-ed. For instance, smiling* is the present participle and *smiled* is the present participle of the verb *smile.*

A participial phrase is a word group that includes a present participle (such as *smiling*) or a past participle (such as *smiled*) and a modifier, object, and/or complement. It often functions as an adjective.

A participial phrase at the beginning of a sentence must refer to the grammatical subject of the sentence. In the following sentence, the word walking refers to the subject (*he* saw), not to the woman:

**Walking down the street, he saw** a woman and a child.

To make the phrase refer to the woman, you need to rewrite the sentence:

**He saw a woman and a child walking** down the street.

The same rule applies to participial phrases preceded by a conjunction, a preposition, nouns in apposition (written side by side), adjectives, and adjective phrases if they begin the sentence.

Ignoring this rule may result in sentences with unintended meanings which are confusing or ridiculous.

Being in a dilapidated condition, Bob was able to buy the house very cheap.

The subject of this sentence is *Bob;* the participial phrase functions as an adjective that applies to the subject. So, Bob is in a dilapidated condition, and because of that, he was able to buy a house very cheap. The sentence must be rewritten to make sense.

## 5.04 | **Active voice and passive voice.**

Writers are often told to use active voice, but many don't understand what this means or how to do it. *Active voice* tells the reader who is responsible for an action, and the doer performs the action of the verb. This next sentence is written in active voice. The woman is the doer; the action is clearing dishes from the table.

Judith cleared the dishes from the table.

In passive voice, the object acted upon is the subject of the sentence. Using the same sentence but writing in passive voice, the object acted upon—the dishes—is the subject, and the doer is mentioned in a prepositional phrase at the end, almost as an afterthought.

> The dishes were cleared from the table by Judith.

Sentences written in passive voice can be confusing and may contribute to word clutter. The above sentence has ten words; the first sentence, written in active voice, has only eight words. Writing in active voice helps to eliminate word clutter. The resulting sentence is usually stronger and more direct:

> I shall always remember my first visit to Boston.

This is much better than the passive-voice construction:

> My first visit to Boston will always be remembered by me.

This latter sentence is less direct, and the wording is awkward. If we try to make it more concise by omitting "by me," we introduce ambiguity.

> My first visit to Boston will always be remembered.

Who will remember the visit—the writer, the citizens of Boston, someone not mentioned, or the world at large?

## 5.05 | When passive voice is appropriate.

Although passive voice should be used sparingly, it is sometimes the appropriate choice. Use passive voice when you want to emphasize the action or object of the action rather than the doer.

> After much debate, the resolution was adopted by the leaders of the Mars colony.

In this sentence, the emphasis is on the action—a resolution was adopted. The leaders of the Mars colony who performed the action are of secondary importance. Here are a few more examples of active- and passive-voice constructions:

> **Passive:** During the class, the story was critiqued by the writers.

**Active:** The writers critiqued the story during the class.

**Passive:** In the computer code, a virus was hidden by the angry programmer.

**Active:** The angry programmer hid a virus in the computer code.

In some passive-voice sentences, the doer is unknown or unimportant. If it does not matter who did an action, and the action is the main point you want to emphasize, the passive construction may be appropriate:

The meeting was held at 1 p.m. in the local library.

Gina's house was robbed sometime last night.

In the sentences above, the passive verbs *was held* and *was robbed* indicate actions, but the doers of the actions are not mentioned; thus, both sentences are written in passive voice. In the first, the main point is that the meeting was held, and who organized it isn't important. In the second, the person who robbed Gina's house is unknown.

Here are other reasons it might be appropriate to use passive voice:

- To establish an authoritative tone:

  Visitors *are* **not allowed** in the museum after 6 p.m.

- To maintain the focus on the subject throughout a passage:

  The director of the Mars colony presented a controversial plan to euthanize all settlers over the age of 50. After hours of debate, the proposal **was endorsed** by a majority of the council.

- To be tactful by not naming a doer responsible for the action:

  The window **was** somehow **broken**.

## 5.06 | Avoid switching from active to passive voice.

Avoiding switching from an active verb in the first part of a sentence to a passive verb in the remainder of the sentence. The effect is usually awkward and confusing.

✗ Jason disliked being married, so his wife and two children are abandoned by him.

☺ Jason disliked being married, so he abandoned his wife and two children.

## 5.07 | Avoid impersonal passive expressions.

Avoid impersonal passive expressions (passive verbs with the word *it* as the subject). Sentences with these constructions are almost always awkward, impersonal, and uninformative. Instead, write the sentence with a subject and make the verb active, as in the following examples:

| ✗ Impersonal passive | ☺ Subject + active verb |
| --- | --- |
| It can be seen that | We can see that |
| It has been decided that | Someone has decided that |
| It was recommended that | We recommend that |
| It is said that | The activists have said that |
| It was reported that | The officer concluded that |
| It must be considered that | One must consider that |

In a few situations, you may have a specific reason for using impersonal passive constructions, such as in technical or scientific writing.

If you are uncertain of the person or thing performing the action, write the sentence using a general noun or pronoun (e.g., *one, someone, somebody, people*).

## 5.08 | Avoid overuse of passive constructions.

In scientific, technical, and legal writing where it may be appropriate to use passive-verb constructions, be careful that you don't overuse passive voice when you describe a process. Try to keep verbs active by indicating who did the various tasks you are describing. In the first example below, all the verbs are passive and the reader has no idea who performed the actions. To make the paragraph more informative and easier to read, supply nouns to identify the doers and make the verbs active, as shown in the second example:

✗ First, the length and width of the lot were measured. Then the height of the trees was determined. While that was going on, the trash on the lot was picked up and thrown into a dumpster.

☺ First, the surveyor measured the length and width of the lot. Then, his assistant determined the height of the trees. While they did that, the cleanup crew picked up the trash on the lot and threw it into a dumpster.

Whenever you write proposals or recommendations in a technical or legal documents, try to limit passive constructions as much as possible. Use the active voice and indicate who should carry out the recommended action or instruction.

✗ **It is recommended that the property owner be ordered** to demolish the derelict building because it is a fire hazard.

☺ **We recommend that the City Attorney order** the property owner to demolish the derelict building because it is a fire hazard.

✗ **Something must be done** to stop the spread of the Zika virus.

☺ **State and county health departments must do something** to stop the spread of the Zika virus.

## 5.09 | Avoid passive verb forms *to use* and *to do.*

Avoid the sloppy habit of relying on the passive tenses of the verbs *to use* and *to do*. The passive constructions are almost always awkward and less concise. Note the following examples of passive verbs forms and the suggested alternatives:

✗ This pump is **used to** cool the nuclear reactor.

☺ This pump **cools** the nuclear reactor.

✗ The bookkeeping **is done** by Alice.

☺ Alice **does** the bookkeeping.

✗ The sorting of the nuts and bolts **was done** by Kevin.

☺ Kevin **sorted** the nuts and bolts.

✗ **The car was used** to commit a string of robberies by the suspect.

☺ The suspect **used the car to commit** a string of robberies.

# Chapter 6
## Nouns—People, Places, Things

### 6.01 | Proper and common nouns.

A *noun* is a word that names something. It can be a person's name, a place, a thing, or an abstract quality such as justice, truth, or happiness. A proper noun names a particular or special place, person (or people), or thing. A proper noun is always capitalized (America, Joseph, Italy, Microsoft, etc.) A common noun is a general or class noun that names an object or abstract quality, and it is written in lower-case.

### 6.02 | Forming plural nouns.

A *singular* noun refers to one of something, a *plural* noun refers to more than one. Plurals of singular nouns are formed based on specific rules, with a handful of exceptions.

**1.** For most nouns, add *s* to the singular: car+s = *cars*; house+s = *houses*; war+s = *wars*.

**2.** For most nouns ending in *s, ch, sh,* or *x,* add *es* to the singular: box+es = *boxes*; dish+es = *dishes*; class+es = *classes*; watch+es = *watches*.

**3.** For nouns ending in *y* preceded by a vowel (a, e, i, o, u), add *s* to the singular: boy+s = *boys*; pray+s = *prays*; valley+s = *valleys*. Two exceptions: soliloquy = *soliloquies*, and colloquy = *colloquies*.

**4.** For nouns ending in *y* preceded by a consonant (any letter other than a vowel), change the *y* to *i* and add *es:* army = *armies*; pony = *ponies*; sky = *skies*.

**5.** For most nouns ending in *f* or *fe*, add *s* to the singular: cliff+s = *cliffs*; knockoff+s = *knockoffs*; safe+s = *safes*.

However, a few nouns change *f* or *fe* to *v* and add *es*: wife = *wives*; self = *selves*; half = *halves*. Others include: *calf, elf, half, knife, leaf, life, loaf, sheaf, shelf, thief, wharf, wife, wolf.* (*Wharf* has also a plural, *wharfs*.)

**6.** For most nouns ending in *o*, add *s* to the singular: cameo+s = *cameos*. But for some nouns ending in *o* and preceded by a consonant, add *es*: volcano+es = *volcanoes*. Other nouns in this class are: *buffalo, cargo, calico, echo, embargo, flamingo, hero, motto, mulatto, potato, tomato, tornado, torpedo, veto.*

**7.** The following common nouns always form their plurals in an irregular way: appendix = *appendices*; cactus = *cacti*; child = *children*; foot = *feet*; goose = *geese*; louse = *lice*; man = *men*; mouse = *mice*; ox = *oxen*; person = *people*; tooth = *teeth*; woman = *women*.

**8.** *Compound nouns* are formed by the union of two words, either two nouns or a noun joined to a descriptive word or phrase. The principal noun of a compound noun, whether it precedes or follows the descripttive part, is usually the noun that changes to form the plural: attorneys general, mothers-in-law, sergeants major, passersby, doctors of philosophy.

**9.** For some compound nouns joined by a hyphen, add *s* at the end of the second noun that follows the hyphen: grown-ups, go-betweens, good-for-nothings.

**10.** Proper names and titles generally form plurals in the same way as do other nouns: Senators Pence and Kaine, the three Roberts.

**11.** Some nouns are the same in both the singular and plural form: deer, offspring, salmon, shrimp, spacecraft, swine, etc.

**12.** Some nouns used in two senses have two different plural forms. The most important are the following:

| brother | brothers (by blood) | brethren (fraternal) |
|---------|---------------------|----------------------|
| die | dies (for coinage) | dice (for games) |
| fish | fishes (separately) | fish (collectively) |
| genius | geniuses (brilliant men) | genii (mythical beings) |
| head | heads (of the body) | head (of cattle) |
| index | indexes (of books) | indices (in algebra) |

## 6.03 | Forming possessive nouns.

The *possessive case* is the form used to show ownership. Possession is indicated by inserting an apostrophe in the noun, based on a series of punctuation rules. These rules are fairly complex and discussed at length in Chapter 21, *Apostrophes and Possessives*.

## 6.04 | Gender and nouns.

*Gender* in grammar is the quality of nouns or pronouns that denotes the sex of the person or thing represented. Nouns and pronouns that refer to males are said to be masculine gender, and those referring to females are feminine gender. Nouns that refer to things without sex are in the neutral gender.

With nouns, gender is of little concern. The only variation is the addition of the syllable *ess* to certain masculine nouns to signify a change to the feminine gender (actor to actress; author to authoress). However, most contemporary style guides suggest that feminine-gender nouns be avoided and the stem nouns be used instead. Instead of writing *actress*, write *She is a talented actor*; instead of *authoress*, write *She is the author of five books*, and so on.

## 6.05 | Avoid noun strings.

Often, when a writer attempts to be brief by stringing nouns together, confusion results. Compare the meaning of the original sentences below with the intended meaning in the revisions.

X We must modernize our obsolete **nuclear weapons tracking system**.

☺ We must modernize our **system for tracking obsolete nuclear weapons**.

✗ We must revise our **foreign check cashing rules**.

☺ We must revise our **rules for cashing foreign checks**.

## 6.06 | Repeat the full noun.

Don't omit words in a proper noun to make the list shorter. Include all the words in the proper noun to be clear.

✗ North and South Carolina

☺ North Carolina and South Carolina

✗ Central and West Africa

☺ Central Africa and West Africa

## 6.07 | Subject-verb agreement.

Singular nouns take singular verbs, and plural nouns take plural verbs. This advice sounds easy, but it's confusing with collective nouns (staff, family) and when plural words are added between the subject and verb.

✗ The **author** of the books and articles **are**...

☺ The **author** of the books and articles **is**...

✗ The import **level** of corn and wheat **are**...

☺ The import **level** of corn and wheat **is**...

✗ Our **forecast**, together with the computer models, **show** that...

☺ Our **forecast**, together with the computer models, **shows** that...

✗ One key **factor**, high oil prices, **are** the reason...

☺ One key **factor**, high oil prices, **is** the reason...

✗ Our **success** in publishing and marketing books **make** us...

☺ Our **success** in publishing and marketing books **makes** us...

# Chapter 7
## Getting Personal with Pronouns

This chapter presents a detailed overview of pronouns. A *pronoun* is a word that stands in place of a noun. The noun it replaces is called the *antecedent*. This is the short and simple definition. But pronouns can take many forms, and some don't fall into the broad catch-all definition of words that replace nouns.

### 7.01 | **Personal pronouns.**

Personal pronouns replace nouns that represent people. The personal pronouns are: *I, you, he, she, we, they,* and *who.*

> **We** can reach out and explore the stars.

> **I** am excited about writing a novel.

> **He** was a lousy worker and deserved to be fired.

> As Bob and Mary looked outside, **they** saw the thief running away

### 7.02 | **Possessive pronouns.**

Possessive pronouns are forms of personal pronouns that show possession. Typically used as adjectives, they are: *my, your, his, her, our, their,* and *its.*

> I enjoyed reading **his** poem.

> Linda's greatest asset is **her** beautiful smile.

> The kitten enjoyed **its** new toy.

> That idiot stole **my** car!

## 7.03 | **Absolute possessive pronouns.**

Absolute possessive pronouns also show possession, but unlike possessive pronouns, they stand on their own rather than functioning as adjectives. They are: *mine, yours, his, hers, ours,* and *theirs.*

Is this computer **yours** or **hers**?

**His** is the third house on the left.

Our cat is asleep on the porch, so it must be **theirs**.

## 7.04 | **Relative pronouns.**

Relative pronouns are words that connect a clause or a phrase to a noun or pronoun and usually add more detail to a sentence. The relative pronouns are: *who, whoever, whom, whomever, whose, which, that, where;* and sometimes *but* and *as.*

The man **who** stole the car was arrested.

Ice cream, **which** we all enjoy, melts quickly in the summer.

This is the movie **that** everyone is talking about.

## 7.05 | **Demonstrative pronouns.**

Demonstrative pronouns are used to demonstrate or indicate something. They usually take the place of a noun phrase. The demonstrative pronouns are: *this, that, these, those,* and *such.*

**This** is the book I want to read.

**Those** are the workers who were fired.

**These** trees are taller than **those**.

## 7.06 | **Indefinite pronouns.**

Indefinite pronouns are similar to demonstrative pronouns but refer to something vague or non-specific. Indefinite pronouns include: *all, another, any, anybody, anyone, anything, each, either, everybody, everyone, everything, few, many, no one, nobody, none, nothing, one, several, some, somebody,* and *someone.*

We are **all** in the gutter, but **some** of us are looking at the stars.
—Oscar Wilde

**Everyone** has gone to the park.

I called the cable company, but **nobody** answered.

## 7.07 | Interrogative pronouns.

Interrogative pronouns are typically used in sentences that ask questions. These words don't replace nouns per se but stand in for a noun that is unknown or undefined. The interrogative pronouns are: *who, whoever, whom, whomever, which, whichever, what, whatever, where,* and *wherever.*

**Who** told you to call me?

**Which** man is taller?

**Whose** computer is that?

**Whom** do you live with?

## 7.08 | Reciprocal pronouns.

Reciprocal pronouns are words that express a mutual action or relationship between two or more people. The two reciprocal pronouns are: *one another* and *each other.*

Melinda and Kate have disliked **each other** for years.

The writers helped **one another** in the workshop.

**TIP:** As a general rule, use *each other* when the sentence involves two people, and use *one another* when three or more people are involved in the reciprocal action.

## 7.09 | Reflexive pronouns.

Reflexive pronouns are words that end in *self* or *selves* and are preceded by a noun, pronoun, adjective, or adverb to which it refers (usually the subject of the sentence). The reflexive pronouns are: *myself, yourself, herself, himself, itself, yourselves, ourselves,* and *themselves.*

I can't lift it by **myself.**

She chided **herself** for being timid.

I wish your kids would behave **themselves**.

## 7.10 | Intensive (emphatic) pronouns.

Intensive pronouns use reflexive pronouns to add emphasis to a noun or another pronoun, usually the subject of the sentence. These pronouns include: *myself, himself, herself, themselves, itself, yourself, yourselves,* and *ourselves*.

Maria washed the dishes **herself.**

I **myself** like stargazing on a warm summer night.

The cat caught the mouse **itself**.

Joe and Molly remodeled the house **themselves**.

✳ **TIP:** If you omit an intensive pronoun, the sentence will still make sense. But if deleting the pronoun turns the sentence into a fragment or renders it unintelligible, then the word may be a reflexive pronoun.

## 7.11 | Avoid pronoun-noun confusion.

A pronoun must clearly refer to a particular noun (called its *antecedent*) for the sentence to make sense. Generally, it should refer to the closest noun that precedes it. When the reference to a noun is awkward or ambiguous, the sentence may be confusing, as the following:

✗ Charles sent a box of cheese, and **it** was made of wood.

Many writers misuse pronouns in this way and introduce ambiguity into their sentences. With relative clauses, this error can be avoided often by placing the relative clause as near as possible to the noun it limits.

☺ Charles sent cheese in a box made of wood.

☺ Charles sent a box of cheese, and *the box* was made of wood.

Note the following sentence:

✗ A cat jumped into the **yard which wore** a blue ribbon.

This construction implies that the yard wore a blue ribbon, which makes no sense. We could rewrite the sentence to read:

☺ **A cat, which wore** a blue ribbon, jumped into the yard.

Sometimes, a pronoun isn't needed and can be trimmed. Let's eliminate the pronoun *which* and improve the flow of the sentence:

☺ **A cat wearing** a blue ribbon was found in the yard.

Compound subjects can cause similar headaches for writers. Consider this sentence:

✗ Mr. Adams and Mr. West arrived together. **He** is my boss.

The pronoun *He* in the second sentence is ambiguous because there's no indication of whether it refers to Mr. Adams or Mr. West. If there is any doubt about the meaning, omit the pronoun and repeat the noun:

☺ Mr. Adams and Mr. West arrived together. **Mr. Adams** is my boss.

Do not use a pronoun to indicate a noun that has not been specifically used as a noun in the previous clause or sentence.

## 7.12 | Singular and plural noun/pronoun agreement.

Pronouns must agree with the nouns they reference. A plural antecedent requires a plural pronoun, and a singular antecedent requires a singular pronoun.

✗ **Employees** must hand in **his** time cards on Friday.

☺ **Employees** must hand in **their** time cards on Friday.

✗ That **boy** must turn in **their** homework.

☺ That **boy** must turn in **his** homework.

When you use a singular noun, make sure all the pronouns that follow in the sentence and reference that noun are singular as well.

> ✗ The **man** brought his hammer and saw. **He** forgot to bring nails, so **he** went back to **their** shop to pick some up.

> ☺ The **man** brought his hammer and saw. **He** forgot to bring nails, so **he** went back to *his* shop to pick some up.

If a sentence seems awkward, or if you want to avoid the use of gender-specific pronouns, replace the singular noun with a plural noun, and then use a plural pronoun.

> Singular:
>
> A **worker** should be paid for **his** overtime work.

> Plural:
>
> **Workers** should be paid for **their** overtime work.

## 7.13 | Gender issues and pronouns.

In the past, it was common practice to use pronouns of the male form when referring to general nouns associated with traditionally masculine qualities, and to use pronouns of the female form for nouns associated with feminine qualities (as well as ships, airplanes, and countries). More recently, the trend has been to use masculine pronouns for all general nouns unless a noun has a distinct feminine bias: *He broke the window. The car belongs to him. The lipstick was in her purse.* Because lipstick is more commonly associated with females, the noun *lipstick* takes a feminine-gender pronoun. These writing styles have fallen out of favor and should be avoided as much as possible.

As a workaround, some writers have begun using the plural pronoun *their* as a singular, gender-neutral pronoun. For example: *Every student must turn in their homework.* However, this approach becomes problematic when the plural pronoun *they* is used in the singular form and substituted for other tenses, which results in faulty syntax such as: *"Tell that worker they must be careful on the roof."*

Also, this approach runs counter to *Chicago Manual of Style,* which states that the expressions *he or she* and *his or her* should be used instead.

> Every student must turn in **his** *or* **her** homework.

To avoid this clumsy construction, Chicago Style suggests the sentence be rewritten to eliminate gender-specific pronouns:

> Homework must be turned in by every student.

Here are some other general pointers to follow in this regard:

When writing about people in general, try to use plural nouns (e.g., people, workers, etc.) whenever possible so that you can also use plural, gender-neutral pronouns such as *they, their, and them* can be used.

If you must use singular pronouns to refer to people in general, alternate between the masculine and feminine pronoun forms. Use *he, him, his, himself* in one paragraph, and switch to *she, her, hers, herself* in the next. To avoid confusing the reader, never switch in the same paragraph.

Avoid overuse of the compound expressions "he or she," "him and her," and so on, even though this syntax is suggested by *CMOS.* Occasional use of these expressions is acceptable, but overuse is likely to become tedious for readers and should be avoided. Never use strange or obscure abbreviations like *he/she, s/he, (s)he, him/her,* or *himself/herself.*

## 7.14 | *Group nouns and pronoun agreement.*

Group nouns, or collective nouns, are words that refer to groups of more than one person: army, audience, class, family, police, staff, team, among others. Some group nouns are singular; others are plural. Some can be used either way at the writer's discretion. Always match pronoun references to the noun form you are using and be consistent. If you treat a group noun as singular, keep the verb and pronoun references to it singular too.

☺ The **jury** has delivered **its** verdict.

☺ The **police** have found **their** suspect, and **they** arrested him.

In most cases, if you are not sure whether to make a group noun singular or plural, add the expression "members of" before the noun and then use plural pronouns. For example, with the group noun "the committee," *members of the committee* is clearly plural, so you can write:

☺ The **members** of the committee postponed **their** meeting.

## 7.15 | Compound nouns and pronouns.

Two or more antecedents connected by the conjunctions *or* or *nor* are often mistakenly treated as plural when the singular should be used.

✗ Neither John **nor** James brought **their** books.

☺ Neither John **nor** James brought **his** books.

When a pronoun has two or more singular antecedents connected by *or* or *nor,* the pronoun must be singular number. But if one of the antecedents is plural, then the pronoun must also be in the plural:

Neither Sarah **nor her children** opened **their** gifts.

When a pronoun has two or more singular or plural antecedents connected by the word *and,* the pronoun must be plural:

**Jack and Jill** carried **their** books up the hill.

## 7.16 | Compound personal pronouns.

Compound personal pronouns are formed by adding *self* or *selves* to certain objective and possessive personal pronouns: *myself, herself, himself, itself, themselves,* etc. These words add emphasis to an expression.

I, **myself**, did it,

He, **himself**, said so.

Compound personal pronouns also can be used reflexively after verbs and prepositions.

> He mentioned **himself**.

> He did it for **himself**.

Compound personal pronouns have no possessive forms. But for emphasis, the word *own* with the ordinary possessive form may be used:

> I have my **own** book.

> Bring your **own** work.

> He has a home of his **own**.

### 7.17 | Avoid unnecessary personal pronouns.

Avoid the use of personal pronouns where they are unnecessary. As a rule of thumb, when a proper noun and a personal pronoun appear side by side in a sentence, the pronoun is unnecessary and can be omitted.

> ✗ Jason, **he did** it—call the police!

> ☺ **Jason did** it—call the police!

> ✗ **Brenda, she said** the man was spying on her.

> ☺ **Brenda said** the man was spying on her.

### 7.18 | Compound subjects and the pronoun *I*.

The pronoun *I* should always be capitalized, and when used as part of a compound subject, it should always be placed second.

> ✗ **I and Karen** went to the beach.

> ☺ **Karen and I** went to the beach.

### 7.19 | Avoid using *you* and *your* as indefinite pronouns.

In technical and news writing, unless you are presenting instructions for the reader to follow, avoid using the pronouns *you* and *your* to mean anyone in general. Use a more specific noun or pronoun, or use *we*.

✗ In this story, **you** can see how politicians play on **your** fears.

☺ In this story, **readers** can see how politicians play on **their** fears.

☺ In this story, **we** can see how politicians play on **our** fears.

## 7.20 | Avoid using *it* as a general pronoun.

Avoid the sloppy use of *it* as a general pronoun. This is a very common mistake. Instead of writing, for example, "It says in this book…" write "This book says…"

Likewise, avoid awkward expressions such as "By presenting the facts in this way, it helps the reader…" Instead write: "Presenting the facts in this way helps the reader…"

Often, you can eliminate the unnecessary use of the word *it* with an adverb or by rewriting a sentence more concisely, as in these examples:

| ✗ Avoid this expression | ☺ Replace with |
| --- | --- |
| It is clear that… | Clearly… |
| It is obvious that… | Obviously… |
| It was impossible for her to… | She could not… |
| It is essential for students to… | Students must… |

Make sure that when you do use the pronoun *it*, the reader understands clearly what the word refers to. Do not use *it* to refer to a complete idea in the previous clause; like other pronouns, *it* must have a specific antecedent. When in doubt, repeat the noun.

## 7.21 | The noun *person* is always singular.

Be careful with the word *person*—it is always singular and requires singular pronoun references. Do not follow the word *person* with plural pronouns (*they, their, them*) or a plural verb. If you want the pronouns and verbs to be plural, use the word *people* instead. If you want to retain the word *person*, select an appropriate singular pronoun (*he, him* or *she, her*) and keep the verbs singular.

## 7.22 | Using the pronoun *this.*

One pronoun that causes trouble for writers is the word *this*. Avoid using the word on its own to refer to an entire idea in the previous sentence. If the pronoun does not refer to a specific noun in the previous sentence, use a noun with it to clarify the sense.

✗ I placed last in the race. **This upset me** considerably.

☺ I placed last in the race. **This <u>result</u> upset me** considerably.

✗ When Sue found her purse stolen, **this angered** her.

☺ When Sue found her purse stolen, **this <u>discovery</u> angered her**.

In both of these examples, *this* refers to the entire idea in the previous clause, not to a specific noun in the sentence. Avoid using the word *this* in this manner. Instead, supply a noun to go with it.

## 7.23 | Using *but that* and *but what.*

Use *but that* when the word "but" is a conjunction and *that* introduces a noun clause, as in the following:

There is no doubt **but that** he will be upset.

Use *but what* when "but" is a preposition in the sense of "except":

He has no money **but** *(except)* **what** his father gave him.

## 7.24 | *Them* versus *those.*

*Them* is a pronoun and should never be used as an adjective. *Those* is the adjective that should be used in its place.

✗ **Them people** are breaking the law. Arrest them!

☺ **Those people** are breaking the law. Arrest them!

✗ **Them** were the dogs I saw running loose.

☺ **Those** were the dogs I saw running loose.

## 7.25 | Each, every, and everybody

The following words are usually singular and require a singular pronoun: *each, every, somebody, someone, anyone, everyone,* and *everybody.* Avoid getting into the bad habit of routinely using these words with plural pronouns (e.g., they, their).

✗ **Each** athlete must carry **their** own luggage.

☺ **Each** athlete must carry **his** own luggage.

✗ **Everybody** must complete **their** own work to pass the class.

☺ **Everybody** must complete **his or her** own work to pass the class.

If the "his or her" construction is awkward in your sentence or you want to avoid using pronouns which mention gender, you should rewrite the expression as a plural phrase. Use the word *all* or a plural general noun such as *people* or *students,* and use a plural pronoun.

**All** athletes must carry **their** own luggage

**People** are always responsible for **their** own actions.

**Students** must hand **their** work in to pass the course.

## 7.26 | Who, whom, and whose.

The pronoun that causes the most difficulty for many writers is the relative and interrogative pronoun (*who, whom, whose*). When the pronoun is the subject of the dependent clause or question, use *who.* When the pronoun is an object of the verb or a preposition, use *whom.* When the pronoun is a possessive, use *whose.*

Brenda is the student **who** wrote my essay for me.

The politician **whom** I voted for has been arrested.

The man **whose** tools are on the ground fell off the ladder.

Be careful of relative clauses (descriptive dependent clauses introduced by *who, whom, whoever, whomever,* etc.) Choose the form of the word that the dependent clause requires.

>Linda offered a free copy of her book to **whoever** reviews it.

In the above example, *whoever* is the subject of the verb *reviews*, so it has the subject form. *Whomever,* the object form, would not be correct in this sentence.

>She is the defendant **who** the jury found guilty.

The form *who* is appropriate in this sentence because it is the subject of the verb *is*.

## 7.27 | Who, which, and that.

Use the pronoun *who* (with its possessive and objective forms, *whose* and *whom*) when the antecedent denotes a person or people. Use the pronoun *which* when the antecedent denotes animals or things. The pronoun t*hat* may be used with antecedents denoting persons, animals, or things, and it is the correct pronoun to use when the antecedent includes both persons and things.

*That* is known as the restrictive relative because it should be used whenever the relative clause limits the substantive, unless *who* or *which* sounds better.

>He is the man **that did the act.**

The relative clause *that did the act* defines what is meant by *man*. Without the relative clause, the sentence (*He is the man*) obviously would be incomplete.

*Who* and *which* are known as the explanatory or non-restrictive relatives and generally should be used only to introduce relative clauses that add something new to the author's principal thought.

>Spanish, **which is the least complex language**, is easy to learn.

In this sentence, the principal thought is: Spanish is easy to learn. The relative clause, *which is the least complex language*, is a thought; though not as important as the principal thought, is more nearly coordinate than subordinate in its value. It adds a further thought of the speaker that explains the character of the Spanish language. When *who* and *which* are used in this way as explanatory relatives, we see that the relative clause can be omitted without making the sentence incomplete.

Explanatory relative clause:

That book, **which is about history**, has a red cover.

Restrictive relative clause:

The book **that is about history** has a red cover.

Explanatory relative clause:

Lincoln, **who was one of the world's greatest men**, was killed by Booth.

Restrictive relative clause:

The Lincoln **that was killed by Booth** was one of the world's greatest men.

# Chapter 8
## Adjectives and Adverbs

Modifiers are words that describe other words in a sentence, adding to or modifying their meaning. An *adjective* is a word that modifies or gives added description to a noun or a pronoun. An *adverb* is a word that modifies or gives added description to a verb, an adjective, or another adverb. In this chapter, various rules on how to correctly use adverbs and adjectives in your writing will be explored.

### 8.01 | Avoid confusing adjectives and adverbs.

Adjectives and adverbs are closely related in their forms and their use, but do not confuse the two. When you want to modify a noun or pronoun, use an adjective. When you want to modify a verb, an adjective, or an adverb, use an adverb.

George smells **bad**.

☑ *Bad* is an adjective describing *George*; that is, George needs a bath.

George smells **badly**.

☑ *Badly* is an adverb describing *smells*; that is, George's nose does not work well.

I feel **poor**.

☑ *Poor* is an adjective describing *I*; that is, I'm ill or out of money.

I have a headache and feel **poorly**.

📝 *Poorly* is an adverb describing *feel*; that is, my sense of touch is not very good.

To avoid confusing adjectives and adverbs, consider the modifier you intend to use. If you want to write that Ellen says things that are foolish, identify the adjective and adverb forms: *foolish* is an adjective and can only modify a noun or pronoun, while *foolishly* is an adverb and can only modify a verb, an adjective, or another adverb.

✗ She talks **foolish**. (The adjective *foolish* can only modify the pronoun *She*.)

☺ She is **foolish**. (The adjective *foolish* modifies the pronoun *She*.)

☺ She talks **foolishly**. (The adverb *foolishly* modifies the verb *talks*.)

If you want to use the adjective *foolish* in the sentence, you must add either a noun or a pronoun. For example, add the noun *things* and then you could write:

She says **foolish** things.

## 8.02 | *Positioning adjectives and adverbs correctly.*

Make sure that adjectives and adverbs are placed close to the words they modify, so that there is no doubt in the reader's mind about your intent. This rule applies to all phrases that act as adjectives or adverbs.

✗ The man rode **the horse with the red pants** on.

✗ Martha gave the bun to **her sister covered in ketchup**.

In the sentences above, the modifiers are some distance from the words they describe, so they are ambiguous—it seems that the horse is wearing red trousers, and Martha's sister is covered in ketchup.

☺ **The man with the red pants** on rode the horse.

☺ Martha gave her sister **the bun covered in ketchup**.

Put modifiers close to the words that you intend to modify to eliminate ambiguity and confusion.

## 8.03 | *Three degrees of comparison.*

The variation of adjectives and adverbs to indicate the degree of modification they express is called *comparison.* There are three degrees of comparison.

The *positive degree* indicates the simple possession of a quality, such as: true, good, sweet, fast, lovely. The *comparative degree* indicates a stronger degree of the quality than the positive: truer, sweeter, better, faster, lovelier. The *superlative degree* indicates the highest degree of the quality: truest, sweetest, best, fastest, loveliest.

When adjectives and adverbs are compared by inflection, they are said to be compared regularly. The comparative inflection is formed by adding *er,* and the superlative by adding *est.* If the word ends in *y,* the *y* is changed to *i* before adding the ending, as in: pretty, prettier, prettiest.

Most adjectives and adverbs with two or more syllables are compared by using the adverbs *more* and *most;* or, if the comparison is descending, by using *less* and *least,* as in: beautiful, more beautiful, most beautiful, and less beautiful, least beautiful. Some adjectives and adverbs, however, are compared by changing to entirely different words in the comparative and superlative. Note the following:

| Positive | Comparative | Superlative |
|---|---|---|
| bad, ill, evil, badly | worse | worst |
| far | farther, further | farthest, furthest |
| forth | further | furthest |
| good, well | better | best |
| late | later, latter | latest, last |
| little | less | least |
| much, many | more | most |

**NOTE:** *Badly* and *forth* may be used only as adverbs. *Well* is usually an adverb, as in *He talks well*, but also may be used as an adjective: *He seems well*.

## 8.04 | Errors in comparison.

Writers often make errors in comparison. Carefully observe these rules for comparing adjectives and adverbs.

1. Do not attempt to compare adjectives that express absolute quality and cannot be compared: *round, perfect, equally, universal*. A thing may be round or perfect, but it cannot be more round or most round, more perfect or most perfect.

2. Do not use the superlative to compare only two things. Only use the superlative to compare three or more items.

   **X** He is the **largest** of the **two**.

   ☺ He is the **larger** of the **two**.

   ☺ He is the **largest** of the **three**.

3. Make sure your comparisons involve similar items that can be compared. For instance, you cannot compare the cost of living in Canada with America (a geographical area). You can only compare the cost of living in Canada with the cost of living in America.

   **X** The cost of living in Canada is **higher than America**.

   ☺ The cost of living in Canada is **higher than it is in America**.

4. Avoid mixed comparisons. *John is as good, if not better, than she*. If the clause "if not better" were left out, this sentence would read, *John is as good than she*, which is grammatically incorrect. Rewrite the sentence to: *John is as good as, if not better than, she*.

5. When two objects are used in the comparative, one must not be included in the other; but, when two objects are used in the superlative, one must be included in the other.

✗ This machine is **better than any** machine.

☺ This machine is better **than any other machine**.

✗ The discovery of America was more important **than any** geographical discovery. (This says that the discovery of America was more important than itself—an absurdity.)

☺ The discovery of America was more important **than any other** geographical discovery.

✗ He is **the most honest of his colleagues**. (He is not one of "his colleagues.")

☺ He is **more honest than any of his colleagues**; or, He is **the most honest of all** the colleagues.

Note that after comparatives followed by *than,* the words *any* and *all* should be followed by *other.* But do not use *any* and *other* after superlatives followed by the word *of.*

## 8.05 | Improper forms of adjectives.

The incorrect forms in the following list of adjectives are commonly used in place of the right forms. These expressions should be avoided.

| ✗ Incorrect | ☺ Correct |
| --- | --- |
| nowhere near | not nearly |
| not much or not muchly | not at all |
| firstly | first |
| thusly | thus |
| muchly | much |
| unbeknown | unknown |

## 8.06 | When adjectives and adverbs are alike.

Some adjectives and adverbs are alike in form. Thus, the following sentences both are written correctly:

He works *hard* (adverb).

His work is *hard* (adjective).

In most cases where an adjective and adverb share the same stem, the adverb has an *ly* suffix, as in: *smooth*, an adjective (The track is *smooth*), and *smoothly*, an adverb (The train runs *smoothly*).

## 8.07 | Singular and plural adjectives.

Some adjectives can be used only with singular nouns, and some only with plural nouns. Adjectives such as *one, each,* and *every* require singular nouns, and adjectives such as *several, various, many,* and *two* require plural nouns. In many cases, the noun that the adjective modifies is omitted, and the adjective thus acquires the force of a pronoun. For example: *Few* are seen. *Several* have come.

The adjective pronouns *this* and *that* have plural forms, *these* and *those*. The plurals must be used with plural nouns. Thus, to write *those kind* is incorrect; it should be *those kinds*. Likewise, t*hose sort of men* should be *that sort of men* or *those sorts of men*.

## 8.08 | When to omit adverbs.

Adverbs serve an essential purpose in the English language, giving nuanced meaning and clarity to verbs, adjectives, and other adverbs. Contrary to the musings of Stephen King, who probably was quoting circa 1800s novelist Nathaniel Hawthorne in warning, "The road to hell is paved with adverbs," it is not necessary or even desirable to slash every adverb from your writing. Read any Stephen King novel and you will see a generous sprinkling of adverbs throughout.

Rather than deleting adverbs willy-nilly, a better approach is to include them as needed but avoid overusing them. Make sure that each adverb you use is essential. Follow these simple rules to minimize word clutter and make intelligent use of adverbs:

1. If all or most of the sentences you write contain one or more adverbs, or if words ending in "ly" occur with conspicuous regularity in your paragraphs, it is likely that you have too many adverbs and should remove some of them.

2. Omit unnecessary adverbs in dialogue tags. Write your dialogue so that it reflects your characters' thoughts and moods (show, don't tell). In the sentence below, the adverb *angrily* is redundant and therefore unnecessary. Deborah's anger is clear to the reader both from her words and the fact that she shouted.

✗ "I'm so mad I could scream!" Deborah shouted *angrily*.

☺ "I'm so mad I could scream!" Deborah shouted.

3. Avoid writing multiple adverbs in a single sentence. Instead of writing, "The man stood slowly, smiling evilly, and pointed his finger accusingly," you can remove two of the three adverbs without no loss of clarity:

> The man stood slowly with an evil grin and pointed an accusing finger.

The one remaining adverb (*slowly*) gives the reader a sense of the action and is necessary, since without it, we don't know whether the man stood up slowly, or reluctantly, or jumped to his feet.

## 8.09 | Double negatives.

The expression *I am here* is called an affirmative statement. A denial of that—*I am not here*—is called a negative statement. The words, *not, neither, never, none, nothing, etc.,* are all negative words; that is, they serve to make denials of statements.

Two negatives should never be used in the same sentence, since the effect is to deny the negative you wish to assert. *We haven't no books* means we have some books. The proper negative form would be *We have no books*, or *We haven't any books*. This mistake occurs where contractions such as *isn't, don't, haven't,* etc. are used. Consider these examples in the following sentences:

✗ It **isn't no** use.

✗ **Don't none** of them believe it.

✗ We **didn't do nothing**.

The words *hardly, scarcely, only,* and *but* (in the sense of *only*) are often incorrectly used with a negative. Compare these right and wrong forms:

✗ It was so foggy that we **couldn't hardly** see.

☺ It was so foggy that we **could hardly** see.

✗ There **wasn't only** one man present.

☺ There **was only** one man present.

## 8.10 | Real and really, near and nearly.

Be careful with *real* (adjective) and *really* (adverb); and *near* (adjective or preposition) and *nearly* (adverb). The first member of each pair, as an adjective, must modify a noun or pronoun. The second member of each pair, as an adverb, is the appropriate form if you want to modify a verb, adverb, or adjective.

✗ She has a **real bad** cold.

☺ She has a **really bad** cold.

☺ He **really** did it.

✗ That amount **isn't near enough** money.

☺ That amount **isn't nearly enough** money.

✗ She was **near dead**.

☺ She was **nearly dead**.

☺ She was **near death**.

☺ She had a **near-death experience**.

## 8.11 | *Sure* and *surely*.

Remember that the word *sure* is an adjective, not an adverb. Do not use *sure* to mean *surely* or *certainly*.

✗ **Sure**, reforms are needed, but the issue is exaggerated.

✗ She was **sure** tired after the long climb.

☺ She was **really** tired after the long climb; or,

☺ She was **very tired** after the long climb.

## 8.12 | *Only* and *merely.*

Take particular care with the words *only* and *merely.* They make sense almost anywhere in the sentence, but the sense changes with each position because the word modified by these words changes when you change the position. Notice the difference in sense in these sentences.

**Only the sniper** shot the hostage.

**The only sniper** shot the hostage.

The sniper **only shot the hostage**.

The sniper **shot only the hostage**.

The sniper **shot the only hostage**.

In most cases, place *only* before the word it is intended to modify.

Likewise, the placing of the words *almost, ever, hardly, scarcely, merely*, and *quite* requires care and thought.

## 8.13 | Be careful with the word *unique.*

Be careful with the word *unique*, which means the only one of its kind. Something cannot be more unique or less unique than something else, because an item is either unique or it is not.

## 8.14 | *Coordinate adjectives and commas.*

Coordinate adjectives (adjectives in an interchangeable order) require a comma between each adjective. If the order of the adjectives is not interchangeable, then omit the commas. The adjectives in the following sentence are interchangeable, so commas are required.

He was an *old, dirty, poor, starving* man.

This sentence has no commas because the order of the adjectives is fixed:

She was an *impoverished* **American factory** worker.

## 8.15 | Compound adjectives and commas.

In a list of adjectives before a noun, do not put a comma between the last adjective and the noun. Note the first example in Rule 8.14 above; a comma between *starving* and *man* would be wrong.

## 8.16 | Infinitives that function as nouns.

As explained in Rule 4.01, an infinitive is a verb form that almost always begins with the word "to" and ends with a simple verb, as in: to walk, to speak, to ask. When an infinitive is used as the subject or the object of the main verb, it functions as a noun, and you do not have to worry about anything it might modify.

**To err** is human; **to forgive** is divine.

In this sentence, the two infinitives, *to err* and *to forgive*, function as nouns; they are the subjects of the verb *is*.

## 8.17 | Avoid dangling infinitives.

When you use an infinitive to start a sentence, be sure that it does not dangle but refers to an appropriate noun or pronoun. In the following example, the infinitive *to get* is dangling because the main clause does not contain a clear noun or pronoun that will complete the meaning of the infinitive:

✗ **To get** a good mark, regular attendance is necessary.

☺ **To get** a good mark, **the student** must attend regularly.

Rewrite the sentence as shown to make it clear that we are talking about the student. The same principle holds if the infinitive comes later in the sentence. You still must avoid creating a dangling modifier, a construction in which the infinitive has nothing to complete it. In the sentence below, notice the infinitive *to avoid* does not have any person to refer to.

✗ Extreme care is necessary **to avoid** damage to the machine.

☺ **The operator** must take extreme care **to avoid** damage to the machine.

Rewrite the sentence as indicated so that you make clear to whom the infinitive refers.

## 8.18 | Using participles correctly.

One very common form of the adjective is the *participle*, which is derived from a verb. Every verb forms these verbal adjectives. The present participle consists of the verb stem with -*ing* added, and the past participle commonly ends in -*ed* (although there are many exceptions to this rule). Here are a few examples:

| Verb | Present Participle | Past Participle |
|------|-------------------|-----------------|
| paint | painting | painted |
| study | studying | studied |
| consider | considering | considered |
| tire | tiring | tired |
| enjoy | enjoying | enjoyed |

The participle is an adjective, and therefore a modifier, so it must have a noun or pronoun clearly positioned as the word it describes. Make sure that the sentence does not create confusion by having a participle with no noun or pronoun for it to modify, or placing the noun or pronoun in a position remote from it (dangling participle).

*Bowing* to the crowd, the *bull* caught him unaware.

*Tired* and *staggering, she* was clearly exhausted.

In the first sentence above as it is written, the participle *bowing* logically describes the word *bull*, a noun. If that is not what you mean, then you need to reorganize the sentence to make clearer the connection between the participle and the word it modifies. Similarly, in the second example, the participles *tired* and *staggering* refer to the pronoun *she*. If that is not what you intend, rewrite the sentence to avoid confusion.

Dangling modifiers most commonly occur without any clear word for the adjective to reference. In these next examples, all four sentences contain participles (*considering, cutting, confused, writing*) but no words in the main clause for these adjectives to modify. We have no idea of who is doing the considering and cutting, who is confused, or who is writing. The sentences need to be recast so these adjectives have a noun or pronoun (underlined in the revised sentences) to modify.

   ✗ **Considering** all the evidence, it is clear that she is in the right.

   ☺ **Considering** all the evidence, __we__ clearly see that she is in the right.

   ✗ **Cutting** the weeds, the work was finished in two hours.

   ☺ **Cutting** the weeds, __the crew__ finished the work in two hours.

   ✗ Hopelessly **confused** by this assignment, my essay is a failure.

   ☺ Hopelessly **confused** by this assignment, __I__ wrote a failing essay.

   ✗ **Writing** the horror story in this way, the readers are kept in suspense.

   ☺ **Writing** the horror story in this way, __the author__ makes sure that the readers are kept in suspense.

Remember that in most cases when you start a sentence with a participle ending in *-ing* within the first few words, you will need to provide a word for it to modify very early in the main clause that follows.

## 8.19 | Using gerunds correctly.

Verbs also form verbal nouns called *gerunds*. These are nouns, not participles, but they look like present participles.

**Running** is fun, but **walking** is a bore.

*Running* and *walking* are subjects of the verb *is* in each clause. They are verbal nouns (gerunds). It is not particularly important that you remember the term "gerund", but you should be careful when you use words that end in *-ing*. If they are participles, then they must, like all adjectives, modify a noun or pronoun. If they are gerunds, you must treat them as you would common nouns. Notice, for example, the difference in meaning between the following two sentences:

**I saw him cooking** in the kitchen yesterday.

**I saw his cooking** in the kitchen yesterday.

In the first sentence, the object of the verb *saw* is the pronoun *him*, and the word *cooking* is an adjective (i.e., a participle) describing him, so this sentence means, in effect, "I saw him in the act of cooking yesterday." In the second sentence, the object of the verb *saw* is the gerund *cooking*, which functions here as a noun. So the second sentence means that you saw the cooking he was doing or had done; it does not assert anything about your having seen him.

## 8.20 | *Using gerunds with possessive forms.*

When you use a gerund preceded by a pronoun or a noun indicating to whom or what the gerund belongs, make sure the pronoun or the noun is in the possessive. The following sentences show the possessive noun or pronoun in **bold**, and the gerund is underlined.

**Our** taking the computer without permission is illegal.

Albert is shocked at **Nora's** walking out the door.

The **government's** raising taxes is an unreasonable hardship.

He was surprised at the **woman's** complaining about harassment.

I did not like **Martha's** joking about my car accident.

A possessive before the gerund is commonly required in business and legal correspondence with constructions like the following:

I object to **his** telephoning me with a sales pitch.

I would appreciate **your** sending me the item.

Because of our **manager's** refusing to listen, I quit.

I wish to complain about **George's** managing this project.

## 8.21 | Avoid dangling gerunds.

The same principle that you must avoid dangling participles applies to gerunds. It's not important that you distinguish between gerunds and participles as long as you remember that whenever you start a sentence with a phrase containing a verbal ending in *-ing*, you must make sure that the verbal refers to the first noun it meets in the main clause (usually the subject of the sentence). If it does not, you have a dangling modifier.

**✗ After dancing** all night, **the taxi** took us home.

This sentence infers that the taxi danced all night and then took us home. Rewrite the sentence to include the word *we*, for example, to supply the requisite noun or pronoun for the gerund to modify:

☺ **After dancing** all night, **we went home** in a taxi.

## 8.22 | Passive verbs and dangling modifiers.

If you are in the habit of using many passive verbs, then you will almost certainly write many dangling modifiers, and your style is apt to be quite confusing. To cure the problem, stop writing verbs in the passive voice. The active form usually will eliminate dangling modifiers and make your style better than before.

**✗ After reading** the instructions, the exam was started.

Notice here how the opening verbal modifier, *reading,* is dangling because it has no word to modify in the main clause that follows. In that main clause, the verb, *was started,* is in the passive voice.

☺ After **reading** the instructions, **the students started** the exam.

If you change that main verb to the active form (from *was started* to *started*), and supply a modifier (*students*) in the main clause, the dangling modifier problem disappears.

# Chapter 9
## Trademarks and Service Marks

It is important for writers to understand how to correctly write trademarked names and service marks. In addition, writers must be aware of certain caveats and potential legal consequences when mentioning product names in books and other projects. These basics are spelled out in this chapter.

A *trademark* gives a business or nonprofit organization the exclusive right to advertise, market and sell a product or service under a particular brand name, logo, or symbol. For example, Microsoft Corp. owns the trademark "PowerPoint," which gives the company the right to market its own software product under this name and to prevent competitors from using the mark on their own products. Infringers can be sued to prevent unauthorized use of the trademark and for monetary damages.

Trademarks are administered by the United States Patent and Trademark Office (USPTO) and similar agencies worldwide. As a condition of approval, the registrant must use the mark in trade or business and meet other criteria, including filing forms and paying renewal fees. Failure to satisfy these requirements may lead to forfeiture of the trademark.

Over time, trademarked names can lose their legal protection. Failure to file the required renewal forms is just one reason this may happen. There are other reasons too, but an in-depth discussion on trademark law is beyond the scope of this book. What matters for our purposes here is that when a trademark falls out of registration, any competitor can use it, and the mark becomes *generic*. For example, "escalator" was a trademark of the Otis Elevator Company some years ago; but it is no longer a protected trademark. So you can write about someone "falling down an escalator" in your book without having to identify "escalator" as a trademarked term, as explained in the rules below.

A service mark is similar to a trademark. But instead of protecting a product name, such as "PowerPoint," a service mark protects a service. For example, the McDonalds$^{SM}$ fast food chain sells hamburgers. The word "hamburger" cannot be trademarked because it is a generic term; but the name of the company that makes and serves hamburgers can be registered as a service mark—McDonalds. It receives the same legal protection as a trademark.

## 9.01 | Consent required to use trademark.

Do not use a trademark or service mark in the title of your book, article, poem, or other writing without the registered owner's consent—and be sure to obtain that permission in writing. Most trademark owners won't allow you to use their mark for a number of reasons, one being that they generally have no control over what you write, and it could reflect unfavorably on their product or business. Another reason is that such use may "dilute" their brand name and weaken the company's trademark protection. Using a trademark in your title without the owner's consent may result in an infringement lawsuit, and you could be liable for substantial monetary damages.

Generally, you may be able to use a trademark or service mark in your title if you are writing an instructional book, a review, or a news story about the product. You can even include criticisms of the product, as long as your comments are unbiased and accurate. Trademark law is not intended to be an impediment to free speech, but rather, it prevents competitors from engaging in unfair business practices and causing confusion that could mislead the public.

## 9.02 | Proper way to write trademark symbol.

If you mention a trademark or a service mark in your book or article, write the ™ symbol or write (TM) after the mark. Do not put a space between the mark and the symbol. If the trademark is officially registered with the USPTO, use the ® symbol instead. For service marks, use the ᔆᴹ symbol, or write (SM) in the same manner. For registered service marks, use the ® symbol.

> She broke into tears, and he handed her a Kleenex™.

> The man asked for a Band-Aid™ for his bloody finger.

> His Burger King™ French fries were quite tasty.

## 9.03 | Avoid disparaging trademarks.

Writing or publishing disparaging remarks about a trademarked product or service may bring legal headaches. Let's say you are writing a horror novel, and in Chapter 2, you kill off everyone who eats Brand XYZ refried beans because the product is tainted with botulism. You personally dislike this brand of beans, so you decide to poke fun at it in your story. Doing so could expose you to legal consequences. You have some protection if you are a writing an expose, a review, or a news story about the product, but the traditional rules of journalism apply, and it may be wise to consult with an attorney before publishing your story.

## 9.04 | Using fictitious trademark names.

In fiction writing, use generic names or make up names that you can use in place of trademarked names and service marks. When inventing a fictitious name, be certain the name you choose is indeed fictitious, and that it doesn't duplicate an existing product!

> She broke into tears and he handed her a Kleenex™.

 Instead of *Kleenex*, use the generic equivalent *tissue*.)

> The man asked for a Band-Aid™ for his bloody finger.

 Instead of *Band-Aid*, use the generic equivalent *bandage*.)

## 9.05 | Trademark names are proper nouns.

Trademarks and service marks are brand names and therefore must be treated as proper nouns. Capitalize the name unless the trademark itself is written in lowercase or mixed case (e.g., iPhone). Do not capitalize a generic name unless it is the first word in a sentence or you use it as a brand name of a fictitious product. Consider these examples.

Buy some *Kleenex™* please.

☑️ *Kleenex* is a trademark, so capitalize it and use the ™ symbol.

*Clorox™* is brand-name bleach.

☑️ *Clorox* is a trademark, so capitalize it.

I rode up the *escalator*.

☑️ The word e*scalator* is a generic name, so write it lowercase.

He likes the black *linoleum* better than the green marble design.

☑️ The word linoleum is a generic name, so write it lowercase.

## 9.06 | Trademarks ruled generic by courts.

The following is a partial list of well-known product names that originally were trademarked but are no longer protected because courts have ruled that the names became generic. You can use these marks in your writing as generic terms in jurisdictions where trademark protection has lapsed, and it is not necessary to identify them as trademarks. Note that some marks retain protection in certain countries while being declared generic in others.

| | |
|---|---|
| Aspirin: | Still a Bayer trademark for acetylsalicylic acid in about 80 countries but declared generic in the United States. |
| Catseye: | Originally a trademark for a specific type of retro-reflective road safety installation. |
| Cellophane: | Still a registered trademark of Innovia Films Ltd. in Europe and other jurisdictions. Declared generic in the U.S. |
| Dry ice: | Trademarked by Dry Ice Corp. of America in 1925. |
| Escalator: | Originally a trademark of Otis Elevator Company. |
| Flip phone: | Originally a trademark of Motorola. |

| | |
|---|---|
| Flit gun: | Originally trademarked as a dispenser for Flit, a brand of insecticide manufactured by Standard Oil Company of New Jersey. |
| Heroin: | Trademarked by Friedrich Bayer & Co. in 1898. |
| Kerosene: | First used around 1852. |
| Laundromat: | Westinghouse trademark, registered in the U.S. in the 1940s (automatic washing machine) and 1950s (coin laundry) now expired. |
| Linoleum: | Floor covering, coined by Frederick Walton in 1864 and ruled as generic following a trademark infringement lawsuit in 1878. |
| Mimeograph: | Originally trademarked by Albert Dick. A low-cost printing press that works by forcing ink through a stencil onto paper. |
| Sellotape: | A British brand of transparent, cellulose-based, pressure-sensitive adhesive tape. |
| Thermos: | A Thermos GmbH trademark name for a vacuum flask; declared generic in the U.S. in 1963. |
| Trampoline: | Originally a trademark of Griswold-Nissen Trampoline & Tumbling. |
| Videotape: | Originally trademarked by Ampex Corp., an early manufacturer of audio and video tape recorders. |

## 9.07 | Trademarks lost for other reasons.

The following is a partial list[1] of former trademarks that have lost protection because of abandonment, non-renewal, or improper issuance (e.g., a generic name existed prior to registration). Some marks retain protection in certain countries while being generic in others.

| | |
|---|---|
| Multiball | Refers to a state on a pinball machine where two or more balls are present on the playfield at once and can be accessed by the flippers. Trademarked by WMS Industries in 1981 as Multi-ball and by Templar Studios in 2000 as Multiball. The latter was abandoned as a trademark in 2001, and the former was canceled in 2002. |
| Touch-tone | Dual-tone multi-frequency telephone signaling. Formerly a trademark of AT&T. |
| TV Dinner | Trademarked in 1953 by C.A. Swanson & Sons. The firm discontinued use of the term in 1962. |
| Webster's Dictionary | The publisher with the strongest link to the original version is Merriam-Webster, but they have a trademark only on "Merriam-Webster." Other dictionaries are legally published as Webster's Dictionary. |
| Yo-Yo | Still a Papa's Toy Co. trademark for a spinning toy in Canada, but a court held that the trademark was improperly issued. |
| ZIP, ZIPcode | Originally registered as a service mark but has since expired. |
| Zipper | Originally a trademark of B.F. Goodrich, used in rubber boots. |

## 9.08 | Trademarks often used but still protected.

The following list shows trademarks that are legally protected, at least in some jurisdictions, but often used by writers in a generic sense. These names are widely known by the public as brand names and are not used by competitors. They are registered trademarks and actively enforced by their owners. *AP Stylebook* advises writers to "use a generic equivalent unless the trademark is essential to the story." The generic alternatives listed in the second column below are suggestions; other generic terms may be equally appropriate.

| Trademark | Generic | Owner |
| --- | --- | --- |
| Adrenalin | epinephrine | Parke-Davis |
| Airshow | in-flight entertainment moving map | Rockwell Collins |
| Armco | crash barrier | AK Steel Holding |
| AstroTurf | artificial turf | Monsanto Co. |
| Auto-Tune | pitch correction | Antares Audio Technologies |
| Band-Aid | adhesive bandage | Johnson & Johnson |
| Biro | ballpoint pen | Société Bic |
| Bobcat | skid-steer loader | Bobcat Co. |
| Bubble Wrap | inflated cushioning | Sealed Air |
| Bubbler | drinking fountain | Kohler Co. |
| Cashpoint | automated teller machine, cash machine | Lloyds Bank |
| Chain gun | motor-operated machine gun | Alliant Techsystems |
| Christmas Seals | Christmas Seals | American Lung Assoc. |
| Cigarette boat | go-fast boat | Cigarette Racing |
| Clorox | bleach | Clorox Co. |
| Coke | cola, soft drink, pop, soda | Coca-Cola Co. |

| | | |
|---|---|---|
| Colt | revolver | Colt Manufacturing Co. |
| Crayola | crayons | Binney & Smith Co. |
| Crescent wrench | adjustable wrench | Crescent Tool Co. |
| Crock-Pot | slow cooker | Sunbeam Products |
| Cuisinart | food processor | Conair |
| Cutex | nail polish | Cutex Brands, Inc. |
| Decora | rocker light switch | Leviton |
| Dictaphone | dictation machine | Nuance Communications |
| Ditto machine | spirit duplicator | Starkey Chemical Process |
| Doll Instant Noodles | instant noodles | Winner Food Products |
| Dumpster | front loader waste container | Dempster Brothers, Inc. |
| Durex | adhesive tape | 3M |
| Esky | cooler | Coleman |
| Fiberglass | glass wool | Owens Corning |
| Filofax | personal organizer | FLB Group Ltd |
| Fix-A-Flat | canned tire inflator | Illinois Tool Works |
| Formica | wood or plastic laminate | Formica Corp. |
| Freon | refrigerant | DuPont |
| Frisbee | flying disc | Wham-O |
| Gib board | drywall | Winstone Wallboards |

| | | |
|---|---|---|
| Glad Wrap | cling-film, plastic wrap | Glad Co. |
| Google | Internet search engine | Google Inc. |
| Hacky Sack | footbag | Wham-O |
| Hills Hoist | rotary clothes line | Hills Industries |
| Hoover | vacuum cleaner | Hoover Company |
| Hula hoop | toy hoop | Wham-O |
| Jacuzzi | hot tub or whirlpool bath | Jacuzzi |
| Javex | bleach | Clorox Co. |
| JCB | backhoe loader | J. C. Bamford |
| Jeep | compact sport utility vehicle | Chrysler |
| Jet Ski | stand-up personal watercraft | Kawasaki |
| Jiffy bag | padded mailing envelopes | Sealed Air |
| JumboTron | large-screen television | Sony |
| Kleenex | facial tissue | Kimberly-Clark |
| Lava lamp | liquid motion lamp | Mathmos |
| Learjet | business jet | Bombardier Aerospace |
| Lexan | polycarbonate resin thermoplastic glass | SABIC |
| Mace | pepper spray | Mace Security International |
| Matchbox | die cast toy | Mattel |

| Memory Stick | flash memory storage device | Sony |
| --- | --- | --- |
| Muzak | elevator music, background music | Muzak Holdings |
| Onesies | infant/Adult bodysuit | Gerber Products Co. |
| Photoshop | photo manipulation | Adobe Systems |
| Ping Pong | table tennis | Parker Brothers |
| Plasticine | modeling clay | Flair Leisure Products |
| Play-Doh | modeling material | Kutol Products - Hasbro |
| Plexiglas | acrylic glass | Altuglas International |
| Pogo | corn dog | ConAgra Foods |
| Popsicle | ice pop; ice lolly (UK) | Good Humor-Breyers |
| Portakabin | portable building | Portakabin Ltd. |
| Post-it | sticky note | 3M |
| Pot Noodle | instant noodles | Unilever |
| PowerPoint | Software application | Microsoft |
| Pritt Stick | glue stick | Henkel |
| Putt-Putt golf | miniature golf | Putt-Putt Fun Center |
| Q-tips | cotton swabs; cotton buds | Unilever |
| Realtor | real estate agent | National Assoc. of Realtors |
| Rizla | rolling paper | Imperial Tobacco |

| | | |
|---|---|---|
| Rollerblade | inline skates | Nordica |
| Rugby | rubber cement | Bostik Philippines Inc. |
| Scalextric | slot car | Hornby Railways |
| Scotch tape | clear adhesive tape | 3M |
| Sellotape | clear adhesive tape | Sellotape Co. |
| Sharpie | permanent marker | Newell Rubbermaid |
| Shop-Vac | wet/dry vacuum | Shop-Vac Corp. |
| Ski-Doo | snowmobile | Bombardier Recreational |
| Stanley | knife; utility knife | Stanley Works |
| Stelvin | closure; screw cap | Rio Tinto Alcan |
| Stetson | cowboy hat | John B. Stetson Co. |
| Styrofoam | extruded polystyrene foam | Dow Chemical Co. |
| Super Glue | cyanoacrylate adhesive | Super Glue Corp. |
| Super Heroes | superhero | DC Comics, Marvel Comics |
| Tannoy | public address system | Tannoy Ltd. |
| Targa top | semi-convertible hard roof panel | Porsche |
| Tarmac | asphalt road surface. | Tarmac |
| Taser | electroshock gun; stun gun | Taser Systems |
| Telecopier | facsimile machine | Xerox |

| | | |
|---|---|---|
| Tipp-Ex | correction Fluid | Tipp-Ex GmbH & Co. |
| Tivoli | amusement park | Tivoli A/S |
| Tupperware | plastic storage containers | Earl Tupper |
| Vaseline | petroleum jelly, petrolatum | Unilever |
| Velcro | hook-and-loop fastener | Velcro Co. |
| Vetsin | monosodium glutamate | Tien Chun Ve-Tsin |
| Walkman | personal stereo | Sony Corp. |
| WaveRunner | personal water craft | Yamaha Motor Co. |
| Winnebago | recreational vehicle | Winnebago Industries |
| Wite-Out | correction fluid | Société Bic |
| Xerox | Photocopier, or to photocopy | Xerox |
| Zamboni | ice resurfacer | Zamboni Co. |

# Chapter 10
## Modern Acronyms

**A**n *acronym* is an abbreviation formed from the initial letters of a short phrase or the name of a company, organization, or agency. Examples of well-known acronyms include FBI, NATO, RSVP, USA, EU, and ASAP. Until comparatively recent times, acronyms were not widely used in the English language. But the scientific advances in recent decades changed the world as well as our languages. The technology revolution in particular, fueled by mass marketing of personal computers and mobile phones, introduced many acronyms into popular culture. Today, almost everyone uses acronyms in verbal and written communication. A knowledge of how to write acronyms and the grammatical rules that apply to them will be helpful to writers across all genres of fiction and nonfiction.

### 10.01 | Capitalized all acronyms.
Write acronyms in all capital letters unless the style guide that you are using directs otherwise or lists exceptions written in lowercase.

> ✗ The **Fbi** agent wanted to interview the suspect **Asap**.

> ☺ The **FBI** agent wanted to interview the suspect **ASAP**.

### 10.02 | Internet and mobile texting acronyms.
A subset of acronyms is used for Internet discussion, online chat, social networking, and mobile phone texting. About five hundred of these acronyms are currently popular, and special rules apply to their use as explained in the rules below. See Appendix A at the end of this book for a complete list of Internet and texting acronyms.

## 10.03 | Internet/texting acronyms case is optional.

Unlike acronyms derived from abbreviated words and names of organizations, and which are written in capital letters, Internet and texting acronyms may be written either in uppercase or lowercase. For mobile texting and online commenting, case is not very important; but for formal writing in news articles, books, and other projects, most style guides recommend that these acronyms should be capitalized. Regardless of how you write them, be consistent: use all caps or all lowercase, and do not switch back and forth. Don't mix cases by capitalizing the first letter and then writing subsequent letters in lowercase.

✗ **FYI**, I expect my **Bff** to text me back **asap**.

✍ Avoid mixed-case acronyms and alternating between cases.

☺ **FYI**, I expect my **BFF** to text me back **ASAP**.

✍ Internet and texting acronyms written in uppercase are okay.

✗ <u>fyi</u>, I expect my bff to text me back asap.

✍ Every sentence must start with a capital letter, even if the first word in the sentence is usually written as a lowercase word.

☺ **Fyi**, I expect my **bff** to text me back **asap**.

✍ Internet and texting acronyms written in lowercase; but if an acronym starts a sentence, that word must be capitalized.

## 10.04 | Spell out acronyms on first use.

Spell out the words or name of the organization from which an acronym is derived on first use in formal writing, and then write the acronym in subsequent references. The following example illustrates this technique: *Federal Bureau of Investigation* is spelled out on first use, and then *FBI* is used thereafter.

The **Federal Bureau of Investigation** spent a full year investigating the drug cartel in Mexico. More than one hundred **FBI** agents were assigned to the investigation.

But do not spell out Internet and texting acronyms on first use; instead, write the acronym.

> ✗ Bob, that's a crazy idea *laughing out loud*!

> ☺ Bob, that's a crazy idea **LOL**!

Do not spell out on first use acronyms that most readers are familiar with in everyday life, such as PC, CD, and DVD.

> ✗ He inserted a **digital versatile disc**. Then, he pressed the "Start" button on the **DVD** player.

> ☺ He inserted a **DVD**. Then, he pressed the "Start" button on the **DVD** player.

## 10.05 | Avoid use of chat acronyms in narrative.

Avoid writing Internet and texting acronyms in narrative and expository passages. Limit their usage to dialogue (in fiction) and direct quotations (in nonfiction)—and then, use sparingly. Occasional acronyms, if any, should blend into your writing and not be so conspicuous that readers notice them. In nonfiction, do not use Internet and texting acronyms at all, except in direct quotations or when such acronyms are themselves the subject of your article, essay, or book.

# PART II
# PUNCTUATION RULES

# Chapter 11
# A Brief History of Punctuation

**P**unctuation allows words to tell their story. The common punctuation marks we use help to clarify the meaning of written language. Without punctuation, everything we write, from simple short stories to novels, news stories, and complex technical and legal documents, would be susceptible to misinterpretation and confusion. Even when punctuation is used but it is used incorrectly, readers are at risk of serious misunderstandings. Short sentences which consist of only a few words can confuse readers when punctuation is not consistently and accurately applied. For example, the meaning of the following sentence depends on the presence or absence of two commas.

The prisoner said the witness was a despicable thief.

The prisoner, said the witness, was a despicable thief.

Punctuation as it exists today is a comparatively recent innovation. The invention of the printing press made it necessary to have a well-defined system for using the various marks that had existed for centuries. For the most part, the personal preferences of scribes had determined how these marks were written. With the dawn of a new era of book reproduction that was quicker and easier than hand copying came the need for a systematic approach to recording and sharing the written word. A system of punctuating those words for the sake of clarity and enhanced understanding was also a necessity.

The earliest writings dating back to the dawn of the Latin alphabet, introduced by the Etruscans in the 8th century BCE, contained strings of letters with no spacing between words or sentences and no punctuation marks of any kind. The first punctuation mark to be used was the dot, or period. Its original purpose was to provide a resting place for the eye and to help a little in grouping the letters into clauses and sentences. It was used at the end of a sentence to indicate abbreviations and as an aesthetic ornament between the letters of an inscription.

Sometimes a slanted mark (/) or a double dot (: or ..) was used to indicate the end of an important section of the writing or even of a sentence. Eventually, spaces were introduced to show the grouping of letters and words. At first, only the sentences were set off by spaces, then the long words, and finally all words.

During the manuscript period, different schools of copyists and even different writers used different marks and systems of pointing. For a considerable time, the location of the dot indicated its force. Placed high (?) it had the force of a period. Placed in a middle position (·) it had the force of a comma. Placed low (.) it had the force of a semicolon.

The foregoing rules were not universally observed, however. A Latin manuscript of the seventh century has a high dot (?) equivalent to a comma, a semicolon used as at present, and a dot accompanied by another dot or a dash to indicate the end of a sentence. A Latin manuscript of the ninth century shows the comma and an inverted semicolon having a value that is used as both a semicolon and colon. Thus, medieval manuscript pointing resembles modern forms in places, but lacks standardization into recognized systems.

The invention of the printing press by Johannes Gutenberg (c. 1398-1468), a German blacksmith, introduced new requirements. Early printers used a period at the end of sentences; the colon; and sometimes the slanting line (/). A reversed semicolon was used as a question mark. Wynkyn de Worde, Caxton's successor in the printing business in London, used five punctuation marks in 1509: the period, semicolon, comma, interrogative, and parenthesis.

The systematization of punctuation is due mainly to Aldus Manutius, who had opened a printing office in Venice in 1494. The great printers of the early day were scholars as well. For years, the main concern of the printer was the sharing of ancient writings with the world, so they were required to be students, critics, and editors of the old manuscripts they printed. They borrowed most of their punctuation from Greek grammarians, but sometimes adapted the meanings. The semicolon, for instance, is the Greek mark of interrogation, or question mark.

The punctuation marks now in use and covered in the following chapters of this book include:

**1.** Comma; separates clauses and phrases.

**2.** Semicolon; separates different statements.

**3.** Colon; the transition point of the sentence.

**4.** Period; marks the end of a sentence.

**5.** Dash (or hyphen); marks abruptness or irregularity.

**6.** Parentheses; enclose interpolations in the sentence.

**7.** Brackets; enclose irregularities in the sentence.

**8.** Interrogation mark; asks a question for an answer.

**9.** Exclamation mark; expresses surprise.

**10.** Apostrophe; marks elisions and the possessive case.

**11.** Quotation marks; set off quoted words and passages.

There are two systems of punctuation in use in the English language, known as the close and open systems. The former uses points wherever possible and of importance in precise composition of every sort, such as laws, contracts and legal documents. The open, or easy, system, omits points wherever possible, and it is used in common forms of composition. The tendency, sometimes pushed too far, is toward an extremely open style of punctuation. The general attitude of writers may be summed up by saying that you must justify the use of a punctuation mark, particularly a comma, rather than its omission.

The chapters in this section of the book provide a detailed overview of the functions of punctuation marks and the everyday rules for their use. Rules for the use of punctuation, however, are flexible, and they are useless unless applied intelligently. No set of rules could ever be devised that would work in every situation or relieve the writer, editor, or proofreader from the necessity of thinking. Writing and editing can never be reduced to an exact science, and the same applies to proofreading and the use of punctuation.

# Chapter 12
## Taking Control of Comma Chaos

**O**ne area of great confusion for writers concerned with the intricacies of punctuation is how and when to use commas. Browse through any book on Amazon or your favorite bookseller, especially self-published titles, and you most likely will find missing or stray commas, even in books that have been edited by professionals.

If you invest just a few hours reading this chapter, and you memorize a set of simple rules, you will be able to conquer the comma chaos in your writing and ensure that your sentences are correctly punctuated. Your readers will thank you, fellow writers will be impressed that you took the time to polish your work, and you will have a book that you can be proud to self-publish or send out to a publisher or agent for review.

Over the years, comma usage has changed, and it will continue to change as the English language evolves. Certain rules pertaining to commas are set in stone; in other cases, comma usage is subjective and may vary from one writer or editor to the next.

A comma indicates a pause. In other words, as you read through a piece of writing, when you reach a comma, it means you should pause for a quick moment before reading the next word. As a practical rule of thumb, you can deduce whether a comma is needed by reading your paragraph and noticing where natural pauses should occur. Consider this sentence published in a popular consumer magazine:

Rachel Ray finds inspiration in cooking her family and her dog.

This construction is flawed and creates confusion for the reader. We can be reasonably certain that Rachel Ray does not enjoy cooking her family and her dog. Read the sentence again, but this time, look for the natural pauses where commas should have been added. Let's rewrite the sentence and add those commas:

Rachel Ray finds inspiration in cooking, her family, and her dog.

Now this statement makes sense and conveys the message that the writer intended.

Read through your current manuscript and apply the same principle—look for natural pauses. Do you have missing commas? If so, add them. Reviewing your manuscript in this manner also will help you spot stray commas that don't belong. As you read, if you find yourself thinking it doesn't make sense to pause where you have a comma, it may be an unnecessary punctuation mark you should remove.

**Remember:** the purpose of the comma is to help clarify the meaning of the words in a sentence, and to prevent ambiguity by clearly showing the separation and relationship of those words to one another. If your readers might find a sentence confusing without a comma, put one in. If your words are clear enough without a comma, you can often omit it. This is a good rule to follow when in doubt.

Let's review some rules of style that you can use to spot and fix comma chaos in your writing. If you learn nothing more from this book than the first two rules below, and if you apply these rules consistently, the quality of your writing will improve noticeably!

## Basic Comma Rules Simplified

**12.01** | Use a comma before the conjunction in a compound sentence containing two or more independent clauses that could be written as simple sentences.

The man left the party angry, and his girlfriend went home with her ex-husband.

Oranges and lemons are in season now, and the grocery store is fully stocked with these fruits.

☑ **TIP:** When in doubt, consider the clauses in the compound sentence. If each clause forms a complete sentence, and the clauses are connected by a coordinating conjunction (*and, or, but,* etc.), a comma is required.

This rule has one exception: If a compound sentence consists of two short sentences, and the sentences are balanced (that is, about the same number of words), a comma is optional. In the two examples below, one has a comma and the other does not. Both are acceptable.

Mark stood up, and Mary sat down.

Mark stood up and Mary sat down.

In the sentence below, the two clauses are imbalanced (one is longer than the other), and in any case, the second clause is not short, so a comma is required.

Mark stood up, and Mary sat down near the open window.

Let's consider one more example. In this sentence, the phrase *sat down again* is not a complete sentence, so Rule 12.01 does not apply—do not use a comma here.

Mark stood up and sat down again.

**12.02** | Use a comma after each member in a series of three or more words, phrases, letters, or digits used with any of the seven coordinating conjunctions: *and, but, for, nor, or, so,* and *yet.*

happy, peaceful, **and** content

The four seasons are winter, spring, summer, **and** fall.

Who doesn't want to be healthy, wealthy, **and** wise?

horses, sheep, **and** cattle; but horses *and* sheep **and** cattle

by the bolt, by the yard, **or** in remnants

Tall, dark, handsome, **but** weird

neither snow, rain, **nor** heat

Are you feeling happy, sad, or just blah?

12 days, 14 hours, **and** 35 minutes (series);

70 years 11 months 6 days (an exception for age)

The above rule applies only if you are using a style guide that requires serial commas, also called Oxford commas. Most publishers, and editors in fiction use *Chicago Manual of Style* (American English) or *Oxford Style Manual* (British English), and both require serial commas. Journalists, Web-content writers and editors working in nonfiction genres often follow *AP Stylebook,* which does not condone serial commas, and if you use them, it's an error. See Rule 12.60 (*What's the Deal with Serial Commas?*) at the end of this chapter for details.

**12.03** | Use a comma after each adjective or adverb in a series of two or more when not connected by a conjunction.

He was a **tall, thin, dark** man.

**12.04** | When two words are combined into a single idea and modified by a single adjective, do not use a comma. But if more than one modifying adjective is present, use a comma on those preceding adjectives.

An old black coat

A bright blue sky

In the above, *black coat* and *blue sky* refer to single concepts. Both sentences have only one modifying adjective (*old* refers to the black coat, and *bright* to the blue sky); therefore, neither requires a comma. But in the next two sentences, *dirty* and *clear* are additional modifiers, so both require commas.

A dirty, old black coat

A clear, bright blue sky

**12.05** | Use commas after each in a series of coordinate qualifying words. This rule is a variation of the preceding rule.

> short, swift streams; but short tributary streams

> fast, cheap motherboards; and fast desktop computers

In these examples, *swift streams* and *cheap motherboards* are not single ideas; *swift* refers to the speed of the water, and *cheap* refers to the price of the motherboards. However, a *tributary stream* is a certain type of stream, and *short* is the only modifier, so no comma. Similarly, a *desktop computer* is a certain kind of computer, and *fast* is the only modifier, so no comma.

**12.06** | When a comma is used with quotation marks, it is always placed inside the closing mark. The same rule usually applies to a period, question mark, and exclamation mark; however, a few exceptions are discussed in a later chapter.

> "Honesty is the best policy," as the proverb says.

> The items marked "A," "B," and "C" were listed in the ad.

> She promised "four," not "five."

**12.07** | Use a comma before quoted dialogue when it is preceded by an introductory phrase or a dialogue tag.

> He said, "Now or never."

> They both exclaimed, "Wait, don't shoot!"

> Patrick Henry declared, "Give me liberty or give me death."

**12.08** | Use a comma to separate two words or phrases where the meaning of the sentence might otherwise be unclear or confusing.

> To Robert, Mark was a jerk.

> Though many people were hungry, eating was not allowed.

> What the strategy is, is a mystery.

**12.09** | Use a comma to indicate the omission of a word or words.

> Lincoln was a great statesman; Grant, a great soldier.

> Then we had much; now, nothing.

In the first example, it is implied that "Grant (was) a great soldier," so a comma is used in place of the omitted verb. In the second example, it is implied that "now (we have) nothing," so a comma is used in place of the omitted words.

**12.10** | As with the preceding rule, use a comma to indicate omission of the verb in a compound sentence that shares a common verb in several clauses. In this example, the common verb is *glories*.

> One man **glories** in his strength, another in his wealth, another in his learning.

**12.11** | Use a comma between an introductory modifying phrase and the subject being modified. In this next sentence, the introductory modifying phrase is italicized.

> **Chased by zombies**, they retreated.

**12.12** | Use commas to set off parenthetic words and phrases. If you don't know what a parenthetic word or phrase is, consider a Grammar 101 refresher to help you correctly apply this (and other) comma rules discussed in this chapter.

> The old man, as a general rule, takes a morning walk.

> It must be remembered, however, that nothing in life is certain.

> The politician's rhetoric might, she hinted, have cost him votes.

> Clark, as we all know, was fired from his job last Friday.

> The novels, which I have read, are definitely worth reading.

> He felt ill, I suppose, after inhaling the fumes.

**12.13** | If the connection of a parenthetical or intermediate expression is so close that it forms a single connected idea, do not use a comma. Similarly, do not use commas to set off a restrictive clause. A restrictive clause functions as an adjective, identifies the word it modifies, and it is essential to the intended meaning of the sentence. Removing a restrictive clause will make the meaning of the sentence unclear.

✗ The computer, nearest the back door, is out of order.

☺ The computer nearest the back door is out of order.

**12.14** | If the connection of a parenthetical or intermediate expression is remote, then set if off using parentheses instead of commas.

The company (formed by Mr. Smith in 2009) lost money for two years and then went bankrupt.

**12.15** | Use a comma between two words or phrases in apposition to each other. The term *apposition* refers to two nouns or noun phrases that sit beside one another, and one identifies or renames the other.

I refer to Merkel, the current leader of Germany.

I have four books by Nora Roberts, my favorite author.

Ms. Baker, the defense attorney, created doubt in the jury's mind.

Alice Baily, Democrat, of Wisconsin

Debbie's sister, Laura, was the youngest. *(Debbie has one sister)*

Jack Cooper, the hijacker, was shot dead.

**12.16** | Omit the comma when an appositive is a single phrase or compound name.

The poet Longfellow was born in Portland.

Democrat Alice Baily of Wisconsin.

Joe's brother Gerald was appointed. *(Joe has several brothers)*

The hijacker Jack Smith was shot dead.

**12.17** | Use a comma to set off words or phrases that express contrast.

> Mr. Fong, not Mr. Adams, won the election.

> The weather was cloudy, not typical of a summer day in July.

> We rule by love, not by force.

> The man was tall, yet shorter than others on his sports team.

In the following example, the phrase *not long after she married him* does not contrast with the first part of the sentence; it adds information to the statement, so no comma.

> She pushed her husband off the bridge not long after they married.

You may, if you wish, omit a comma that sets off a contrasting phrase that begins with *but*. The following sentences are both correct:

> ☺ His wife was quiet but visibly angry.

> ☺ His wife was quiet, but visibly angry.

**12.18** | Use a comma after an interrogative clause when it is followed by a direct question.

> You will call me, won't you?

> You are healthy, are you not?

> You will go to the picnic, will you not?

> Just shut up, will you please?

**12.19** | Do not use a comma before an ampersand (&), even in a list of words in which you would typically use a serial comma.

> Smith, Wesson & Co.

> Red, White & Blue Cafe

**12.20** | Omit commas wherever you can do so without creating ambiguity or confusion in your sentences.

> Executive Order No. 21

Public Law 85-1

He graduates in the year 2016. (never write *2,016*)

My age is 30 years 6 months 12 days.

John Lewis II

Murphy of New York (where only last name is used)

**12.21** | Use a comma after each pair of words in a series of word pairs or phrases not connected by conjunctions.

Sink or swim, live or die, survive or perish.

The meal comes with orange juice and coffee, eggs and toast, bacon or sausage.

This sentence has only one pair of words—*my hand and my heart*—so no comma:

I give my hand and my heart to this vote.

**12.22** | Use a comma to separate coordinate clauses of a compound sentence if the clauses are simple in construction and closely related.

He was kind, not indulgent, to his men; firm, but just, in discipline; courteous, but not familiar, to all.

**12.23** | Use a comma after phrases and clauses placed at the beginning of a sentence by inversion.

After several months of driving, the tires became unsafe to use.

Ever since, she has avoided younger men who drive sports cars.

**12.24** | Introductory phrases that begin with *if, when, wherever, whenever,* and so forth should usually be separated from the rest of the sentence by a comma, even when the statement may appear to be direct.

When an email goes unanswered, it is best to follow up with a copy.

If the book is poorly written, the reader may go on to another.

**12.25** | Use a comma to separate introductory words, phrases, and independent adverbs from the rest of the sentence.

> Now, what are you going to do there?

> I think, also, Franklin is a very honest man.

> This idea, however, had already been debated by others.

**12.26** | Use a comma to separate words or phrases of direct address from the context.

> I submit, gentlemen, to your judgment.

> From today, my son, your future is in your own hands.

**12.27** | Use a comma to indicate an ellipsis, when using an ellipsis would disrupt the flow of the sentence.

> Subscription for the course, fifty dollars.

Very brief sentences, especially in advertising copy, are exceptions to this rule and the comma should be omitted:

> Tickets 50 cents

> Price ten dollars

## Names, Titles, and Locations

**12.28** | Use a comma after a noun or phrase in direct address.

> Officer, was I driving too fast?

> No, Doris, I do not remember.

> Kevin, you frightened me!

> Mr. Smith, I will not answer your dumb question.

> Yes, Mr. Webb, I will re-schedule the meeting.

**12.29** | Use a comma between the title of a person and the name of an organization in the absence of the words *of* or *of the*.

president, University of California

president of the University (no comma, uses of the)

managing partner, Luna Technology Inc.

**12.30** | Omit the comma before name suffixes such as Jr., Sr., Esq., Ph.D., Inc., and so forth, even if the comma is part of the name. But add a comma after a name suffix when it is followed by a title or when other rules apply that would require a comma.

> John Ryan Jr., chairman of the committee, just gave a speech
>
> ✍ but John Ryan Jr. is chairman of the committee.

> Allan Wilson III, London resident, drove into the river.
>
> ✍ but Allan Wilson III drove his car into the river.

> Malibu, CA's waterfront
>
> ✍ or Malibu, California's waterfront

> Motorola Inc. factory workers are entitled to overtime.
>
> Smith, A.H., Jr. (not Smith Jr., A.H.)
>
> John Hale II was elected local sheriff
>
> Mr. Combs Jr. also spoke (where only last name is used)

**12.31** | Use a comma when a full name or a title and a name are followed by a location.

> James Adam Cullen, of Los Angeles
>
> President Faust, of Harvard University
>
> Dr. Robert Greenberg, of Holy Cross Hospital

**12.32** | Use a comma between a person's name and his title or degree.

> Barack Obama, President of the United States

Charles W. Eliot, LL.D.

Rev. Mark McCafferty, Pastor

**12.33** | Do not use a comma between a name and a location when the person is closely identified with place.

Joan of Arc

Henry of Navarre

**12.34** | Use a comma before the word *of* when a proper name is connected with the person's residence or position.

Senator Lodge, of Massachusetts

Professor Smith, of Cal State Northridge

**12.35** | Use a comma after the salutatory phrase at the beginning of a letter, when the salutation is informal (typically, a first name is used). If the salutation is formal, then use a colon.

Informal:

Dear John,

Hi Daniel,

Hey Betty,

Yo dude,

Formal:

Dear Sir:

To Whom It May Concern:

Dear Mrs. Smith:

Ladies and Gentlemen:

**12.36** | Use commas to separate the closing salutation of a formal letter from the rest of the sentence of which it forms a part.

Anticipating your prompt response, I am,

Very truly yours,

John W. Smith

**12.37** | Do not use a comma in bibliographies between the publication name and volume or issue number. But use a comma before the date, if one is listed:

Library of Congress Bulletin 34:238

Library of Congress Bulletin 34:238, April 2016

## Numbers and Dates

**12.50** | Questions about how to write numbers and whether to spell them out or write digits are a source of confusion for many writers. Style guides offer contradictory advice on the subject. For instance:

AP Style: Spell out whole numbers up to and including nine, and write numbers over nine as digits. (Mary has four sons and 13 cats.) Use digits for measurements (2 cups, 12 ounces, 50 pounds, 4 feet, 8 a.m., 65 mph). Spell out numbers in casual expressions, such as: *A picture is worth a thousand words.*

Chicago Style: Spell out whole numbers up to and including one hundred, and write digits for values over one hundred (zero, six, ninety-nine, 101, 1,000). Write digits for measurements (1 cup, 5 yards, 150 pounds). Spell out whole numbers up to and including one hundred when followed by hundred, thousand, million, billion, trillion, etc. (five hundred but 506; six hundred thousand, one million, twenty billion).

Chicago Style Alternate Rule: A second, simplified rule for writing numeric values is similar to AP Style. Spell out whole numbers up to and including nine, and use digits for everything else.

If you adhere to Chicago Style rules, you can choose either option, but be consistent throughout your manuscript. Avoid switching back and forth from one style to the other, as this will give your writing an unpolished quality and may confuse the reader.

**12.51** | Use a comma to set off thousands and millions when numbers over 999 are written as digits.

> Having 4,230 website hits is good, but 1,500,000 hits is better.
>
> He won the election by a margin of 82,614 votes.
>
> The town's 9,681 residents are mostly Republicans.
>
> China's population hit 1,382,106,527 at midnight on June 17, 2016.

**12.52** | Spell out a number at the beginning of a sentence, or rewrite the sentence to avoid awkward construction.

> ✗ 40 residents were evacuated from the collapsed building.
>
> ☺ Forty residents were evacuated from the collapsed building.
>
> ✗ 2016 saw crazy political antics in the U.S.
>
> ☺ The year 2016 saw crazy political antics in the U.S.
>
> ✗ $50,000 is the down payment for the house.
>
> ☺ Fifty thousand dollars is the down payment for the house.
>
> ☺ The down payment for the house is $50,000.

**12.53** | Spell out ordinal numbers up to and including *hundredth* in Chicago Style (first impression, seventy-fifth, 200th). In AP Style, spell out ordinals up to and including *ninth* and write larger ordinals as digits (first, sixth, 12th, 75th). But always use digits when indicating sequence in naming conventions, such as the 4th U.S. Circuit Court of Appeals.

**12.54** | Use a comma to separate two numbers (either spelled out or digits) when the numbers appear in apposition, or side by side, and the meaning of the sentence might unclear or awkward without the comma.

> Instead of dozens, hundreds joined the protest.
>
> Instead of fifty, 300 prisoners escaped from the jail in Italy.

December 7, 1941

In 2016, 800 people fell ill with the disease.

When the clock hit four, 180 soldiers launched an attack.

**12.55** | For calendar years, use the four-digit year. Don't use a comma, and never spell out the year.

The man time-traveled to the year 2895.

August 2016

The year 2000 was a turning point in our lives.

**12.56** | Use a comma after the day and year in a complete date that uses *month-day-year* format when written in a sentence.

The dates of May 20, 2016, to June 22, 2016, were reserved.

This fact was mentioned in the June 13, 2007, report.

**12.57** | Omit the comma when dates are written as month and year, holiday and year, season and year, and with European date format.

June 2015

150 B.C.

Labor Day 2016

February and March 2016

5 January 2006

Summer 2016

Christmas 2017

The same rule applies when dates are written in full sentences.

The weather for May 2016 was fairly close to normal.

The 10 April 2016 registration deadline has passed.

**12.58** | Do not use commas in fractions, decimals, street addresses, telephone numbers, or serial/registration numbers (except patent numbers).

> 1/1500
>
> 5.1947
>
> page 2632
>
> Part No. 189463
>
> 805-555-1212
>
> 6,763,901 B1 (patent number)

**12.59** | Do not use a comma before ZIP code postal designations.

> Santa Barbara, CA 93101
>
> East Rochester, OH 44625-9701

**12.60** | Do not use a comma before compass direction abbreviations.

> 1216 North Sunset Drive NW

## 12.60 | What's the deal with serial commas?

A serial comma, also called an Oxford comma, is used before a coordinating conjunction (*and, but, for, nor, or, so,* and *yet*) in a list of three or more items or conditions. For example, in this phrase, a serial comma is used after the word *oranges:*

> apples, oranges, and pears

Written without a serial comma, the phrase would read:

> apples, oranges and pears

The serial comma isn't only used to separate proper and common nouns. Use it also to separate a list of adjectives (descriptive words), adverbs (words that modify or qualify another word), and even verbs (words that describe actions). For example:

William washed, peeled, rinsed, and tossed the potato in the stew.

The mother spoke to her child quietly, patiently, and lovingly.

The flag was red, white, and blue.

The old, rusty, and broken tool should be discarded.

Without serial commas, these sentences would be punctuated as:

William washed, peeled, rinsed and tossed the potato in the stew.

The mother spoke to her child quietly, patiently and lovingly.

The flag was red, white and blue.

The old, rusty and broken tool should be discarded.

The word *and* is the conjunction used most often to connect the last item to a list, but you would use serial commas before other conjunctions too.

You can laugh, cry, *or* complain about the election results.

Feeling angry, depressed, *but* determined, she filed a harassment lawsuit against her employer.

Whether serial commas should be used will depend upon what you are writing and which style guide you are using. Typically, novels and other works of fiction in the North America follow the punctuation rules given in *Chicago Manual of Style* (American English) or *Oxford Style Guide* (British English)—both mandate serial commas. If you are writing nonfiction, news, or Web content, you will probably use *AP Style*, which states that serial commas should not be used except in rare instances when a serial comma is required for clarity.

Taking a closer look at the debate on serial commas among writers and editors in the U.S. and across Europe, the majority of American English style guides require that the serial comma be used, including *APA Style*, *Chicago Manual of Style*, *MLA Style Manual*, Strunk's *Elements of Style*, and the *U.S. Government Printing Office Style Manual*. But the

*Associated Press Stylebook* and the style book for journalists published by The Canadian Press suggest that it not be used.

The serial comma is not used as often in British English, but some style guides, including *The Oxford Style Manual,* require it. *The Oxford Companion to the English Language* states: "Commas are used to separate items in a list or sequence ...Usage varies as to the inclusion of a comma before and in the last item...This practice is controversial and is known as the serial comma or Oxford comma, because it is part of the house style of Oxford University Press." Some writers and editors use the serial comma only when necessary to avoid confusion and ambiguity.

No matter which style guide you follow, what matters most is that you be consistent. Use serial commas in every instance where they are required, or don't use them at all. Switching back and forth, using serial commas in some sentences and omitting them in others, will give your writing a choppy, unpolished quality that will put off some readers.

Some writers dismiss serial commas, and punctuation in general, as much ado about nothing, and they suggest that readers don't care about punctuation. But repeated surveys have shown the opposite to be true. Negative feedback from readers posted on Amazon.com and elsewhere often mention poor grammar and faulty punctuation as reasons for one- and two-star reviews.

Writers who aspire to impress a traditional publisher or agent, and those who have decided to self-publish, should focus closely not only on plot and content, but grammar, style, and punctuation. A missing comma can change the meaning of a passage in unintended ways. For example, consider the following book dedication:

> To my parents, Ayn Rand and God.

Without a serial comma, this sentence causes ambiguity and confusion for the reader. The above construction suggests that the author's parents are Ayn Rand and God. Obviously, this is not what the writer intended, and using a serial comma eliminates the ambiguity:

To my parents, Ayn Rand, and God.

To use commas correctly, writers must learn and follow specific rules. But it's also important to remember that the purpose of the comma is to separate for the eye what is separate in thought. Commas introduce pauses at the appropriate places and give readers a better sense of the words being read. The comma cannot be correctly used without a thorough understanding of the sense of the words.

# Chapter 13
## Making Sense of Semicolons

Semicolons, like commas, are often misused by novice writers who haven't mastered the basics of English grammar and punctuation. Now that you have familiarized yourself with the rules of comma usage, in this chapter, we will explore style rules for proper use of the semicolon in modern writing.

The semicolon denotes a degree of separation, or a pause, greater than that of the comma, but less than that of the colon or full stop (period). It can help to set off important words in a sentence and enhance readability of complex phrases, especially those with commas, that would otherwise be difficult for readers to follow. Used correctly, the semicolon can help you to avoid overuse of commas, allowing for greater variation in sentence structure and a more interesting writing style than is possible if you rely solely on commas and full stops.

The semicolon is commonly used in longer sentences to connect two or more independent clauses or word groups together to convey a complete thought before ending the sentence with a full stop. Semi—colons have uses in shorter sentences too.

**13.01** | Use a semicolon to replace a period and combine two distinct and closely related sentences into a single thought.

> I bought a new car; it is red with a black interior.

> His book contained typos; he didn't bother to proofread it.

> Don't apologize; you obviously aren't sorry.

> Call me in the morning; you can let me know then.

Bob is in love with Sally; Sally loves John, not Bob.

Eat your dinner; I spent two hours cooking it.

Susan is lousy at math; she failed the exam.

**13.02** | Do not use a semicolon when a dependent clause precedes an independent clause; instead, use a comma.

✗ Although he applied for the job; he wasn't hired.

☺ Although he applied for the job, he wasn't hired.

**13.03** | Use a semicolon to separate phrases or word groups that comprise a list when one or more of the elements contain commas. As an example, the first sentence below makes no sense unless semicolons are used to set off the phrases that contain commas.

✗ Janet attended seminars in Paris, Texas, Rome, Georgia, Madrid, Iowa, Berlin, New Jersey, and other cities as well.

☺ Janet attended seminars in Paris, Texas; Rome, Georgia; Madrid, Iowa; Berlin, New Jersey, and other cities as well.

Robert A. Stone, CEO of Lost Encounters Inc., was a director of Micro Ventures; Leon S. Jones was a Pacific National Bank vice-president and a director of Micro Ventures; Joel N. Gray, chairman of Vista Lending & Co., was also a Micro Ventures director.

**13.04** | Use a semicolon to break up compound sentences for easier reading when the clauses are complex, even if they contain no commas as described in the previous rule.

With ten percent of this flour the bread acquired a slight flavor of rye; fifteen per cent gave it a dark color; a further addition made the baked crumb very hard.

The clinical trial found that seventy-two percent of the volunteers experienced pain relief after taking the medication; eighteen percent reported no relief; the remaining ten percent complained of increased pain after taking the medication.

**13.05** | Use a semicolon to join compound sentences in which the subject of the first clause differs quite a bit from that of the second, and you want to combine them into a single thought.

Marilyn had a fight with her neighbor; the family that lives across the street never argues with anyone.

The power of England relies upon the wisdom of its statesmen; the power of America upon the strength of its military.

In his novel, the author has an earthquake wiping out California; his wife is terrified of earthquakes and won't read the book.

**13.06** | Use a semicolon to separate statements that are too closely related in meaning to be written as separate sentences; also, for contrasting or contradictory statements that you want to connect and express as one thought.

No; we received one-third.

It is true in peace; it is true in war.

War is destructive; peace, constructive.

**13.07** | Use a semicolon to set off explanatory abbreviations and words that explain or summarize the main thought in the preceding matter.

The trade organization represents businesses that manufacture peripherals for desktop computer users; e.g., keyboards, mice, monitors, and flash drives.

Three hotels in Las Vegas offer hefty discounts on rooms during the hot summer months; namely, the Luxor Hotel, Treasure Island, and the Flamingo.

**13.08** | The semicolon can be used to join two short but related independent clauses or phrases to avoid choppiness that would result from writing them as two sentences.

Yes, sir; he did see it.

No, ma'am; I do not recall.

Wait a minute; why did you say that?

I stopped running; I had to catch my breath.

**13.09** | Use a semicolon before a conjunctive adverb such as *however* and *likewise* when it introduces a complete sentence. In most cases, a comma should be used after the conjunctive adverb. A list of conjunctive adverbs is provided below for handy reference.

I asked you to stop; however, you kept doing it.

You wrote two novels; likewise, Sue Ellen wrote two thrillers.

Bring potato chips; also, bring sodas and hot dog buns.

George was pleased by the news; indeed, he was ecstatic.

I plan to live forever; of course, that's not likely to happen.

I don't like that plan; in fact, I think it is a stupid idea.

**List of conjunctive adverbs**

| | | |
|---|---|---|
| accordingly | hence | namely |
| again | however | nevertheless |
| also | in addition | of course |
| as a result | indeed | otherwise |
| besides | in fact | still |
| consequently | in particular | that is |
| finally | instead | then |
| for example | likewise | therefore |
| further | meanwhile | thus |
| furthermore | moreover | |

**13.10** | Do not capitalize common words that follow a semicolon.

✗ I threw the ball; You caught it.

☺ I threw the ball; you caught it.

**13.11** | Capitalize proper nouns that follow a semicolon as you would normally do in a complete sentence.

I bought the cookies; Albert ate them.

You were complaining; I told you to stop and suck it up.

**13.12** | Use a semicolon to indicate chapter references in Biblical citations.

John 9:1-12; 12:3-6

John 9:1-3, 6-12; 12:3-6

## 13.13 | *Can I use semicolons in dialogue?*

Using semicolons in dialogue was frowned upon in the past. American author Kurt Vonnegut considered semicolons in general to be bad form and declared: "Do not use semicolons. They are transvestite hermaphrodites representing absolutely nothing. All they do is show you've been to college."

Everything changes over time, however, including language, as Scottish-American author Gilbert Highet noted: "Language is a living thing. We can feel it changing. Parts of it become old: they drop off and are forgotten. New pieces bud out, spread into leaves, and become big branches, proliferating."

In modern writing and publishing circles, some editors and proofreaders don't like semicolons in dialogue and will remove them; but increasingly, this punctuation mark is finding its way into mainstream fiction. Its use today is common enough that it should be left to each writer to decide based on personal preference and the writer's individual style.

The semicolon can add flexibility and interest to the structure of dialogue when used correctly. As with most constructions, however, moderation is good, but overuse is not. Use this punctuation mark sparingly and only where it fits well. Because it is not seen often in dialogue, overuse may be glaringly obvious to some readers and should be avoided.

# Chapter 14
## The Colon—Not Quite a Period

The colon represents a longer stop than a comma or semicolon, and it is roughly equal to a full stop (period). But rather than indicating the end of a sentence, it joins distinct and related sentences, lists, or phrases into a longer sentence that expresses a single thought. In writing styles of the past, the presence of a colon nearly always meant that a sentence was long and complex. That's not necessarily the case today. For modern writers, the colon offers some flexibility and can be used in various ways, as the examples in these rules demonstrate.

**14.01** | Use a colon at the end of a sentence that precedes a list or group of phrases which refer back to the main statement:

> Four soldiers volunteered for the dangerous mission in the remote mountains of Afghanistan: Jim Bailey, Carl Liston, Ed Williams, and Samuel Adams.

> The boy's excuses for being late to class were: first, his bicycle had a flat tire; second, he did not know the time; third, the older boy who lives next door picked a fight with him; and last, he tripped on a rock and sprained his ankle.

**14.02** | Use a colon at the end of a sentence that precedes a final clause which extends or amplifies the main statement.

> For some people, writing is not a hobby: It is a life calling.

> NATO sent Russia's Putin a clear message: The U.S. and its allies take their treaty obligations to defend Eastern Europe seriously.

Give up conveniences; do not demand special privileges; do not stop work: These are necessary sacrifices while we are at war.

**14.03** | When the details that follow a colon comprise a complete sentence, or if that portion of the sentence begins with a proper noun or proper pronoun, capitalize the first word. Otherwise, write it lowercase.

His wife's kidnapper issued a ridiculous ultimatum: He demanded $10 million, but the victim's family barely can afford to buy food.

✏️  A complete sentence follows the colon, so cap the first word.

There is no question who is qualified for the promotion: Ed Winn.

✏️  A proper noun follows the colon, so capitalize it.

Great writers have one thing in common: imagination.

✏️  The word imagination is not a complete sentence or a proper noun, so write it lowercase.

**14.04** | A colon may be used between parts of a sentence when one or both parts contain two or more clauses divided by semicolons.

Martha wrote four romance novels for young adults; Bob wrote four erotica novels: Martha's were well-written and hit the bestseller list; Bob's were poorly written with many typos, so he should not have been surprised that none of his books sold a single copy.

**14.05** | Use a colon after the formal salutatory phrase at the opening of a letter. When the greeting is informal, use a comma instead.

Informal:

Dear John,

Hi Daniel,

Hey Betty,

Yo dude,

Formal:

> Dear Sir:
>
> To Whom It May Concern:
>
> Dear Mrs. Smith:

**14.06** | A colon can be used to formally introduce any matter that completes a full sentence or question.

> One resident of the drought-stricken city asked: What if we run out water?

> The question remains: Does the Second Amendment give citizens the right to own machine guns and hand grenades?

> The three prerequisites for writing a bestseller are: a great story idea, great writing, and a great marketing plan.

> The 2016 GOP presidential candidate declared: "All of the women on *The Apprentice* flirted with me—consciously or unconsciously. That's to be expected."

**14.07** | A colon can be used at the end of an introductory phrase that precedes a formal quotation.

> After the crowd at the Arizona rally stopped cheering, the GOP presidential nominee vowed: "I will build a great wall—and nobody builds walls better than me, believe me."

> Write a short essay on the following topic: "What is wrong with the global economy?"

> She declared: "We must try to escape from the zombies. If we wait too long, there will be thousands of them, and we will never make it out of this hell hole alive."

But when the introductory clause and the quotation are brief, you may use a comma instead. Doing so is optional and at the writer's discretion.

Mother Teresa said, "Joy is a net of love by which we catch souls."

**14.08** | Use colons to separate hours from minutes and minutes from seconds when expressing clock time.

We met at 2:40 p.m.

12:00:00

**14.09** | A colon may be used before *as, viz.,* and conjunctive adverbs such as *that is, namely,* etc. (see Rule 13.09 for a list of conjunctive adverbs), when these words introduce a series of terms that provide additional detail or clarification about the preceding matter. Also, when a conjunctive adverb is used at the beginning, it is followed by a comma.

The American flag has three colors: namely, red, white, and blue.

Certain vegetables I refuse to eat: peas, broccoli, kale, and turnips.

**14.10** | A colon may be used to separate book titles and subtitles.

*Treasure Hunters: Peril at the Top of the World*

*The Introvert Advantage: How Quiet People Can Thrive in an Extrovert World*

*Biology: The Dynamic Science of Life*

**14.11** | Use a colon to separate the city of publication from the name of the publisher in bibliographic references.

*Congressional Directory.* Washington D.C.: U.S. Government Printing Office

*Apocalypse Orphan.* Vancouver: Spectrum Ink Publishing

**14.12** | Use a colon in imprints before the year, and include a space on both sides of colon as shown below.

U.S. Government Printing Office. Washington D.C. : 2015

Penguin Books. New York : 2016

**14.13** | A colon is commonly used as a separator in Biblical passages and other citations.

> Luke 4:3
>
> I Corinthians 13:13
>
> Journal of Education 3:342-358

**14.14** | The colon may be used in proportions.

> Concrete mixed 5:3:1

**14.15** | A double colon may be used as a ratio sign.

> 1:2::3:6

# Chapter 15
## The Power of the Period

The full stop, or period, is the simplest punctuation mark in the English language. It marks the end of a complete sentence that is not an interrogatory (question) or an exclamatory (expression of surprise or strong emotion). Of Greek origin, the full stop came into use around 300 B.C. The term "period" became popular in the 18th century when printers began using it to refer to a full point—a dot on the baseline of printed matter. By the 1800s, it was synonymous with "full stop" in British English. Today, the term is more prevalent in American English. Besides terminating a declaratory sentence, the period is used in various other ways as described below.

**15.01** | The most common use of the period is at the end of any complete sentence that does not otherwise end with a question mark or an exclamation point.

> Time is money.

> Write with passion or not at all.

> Never, never, never give up.

> He is employed by Microsoft.

> Do not be late.

**15.02** | Use a period after an indirect question or a question intended as a suggestion and not requiring an answer.

> Tell me why you did it.

> What did you expect me to do.

Will you shut up.

May we have your attention.

**15.03** | When a sentence ends with a quotation, use a period inside the closing quotation mark.

I have just read Stephen King's "The Dead Zone."

Karen said to Jill, "I think I need a grammar tutor."

**15.04** | Do not use a period after a quotation mark that is preceded by a period, question mark, exclamation mark, or ellipsis.

✗ Mary said: "Hurry up or we will leave without you.".

☺ Mary said: "Hurry up or we will leave without you."

✗ The teacher asked, "What is your problem?".

☺ The teacher asked, "What is your problem?"

✗ Jim frowned and mumbled, "But I thought...".

☺ Jim frowned and mumbled, "But I thought..."

**15.05** | When a parenthesis closes at the end of a declarative sentence, write the period outside of the closing mark. But see Rules 15.06 and 15.07 for several exceptions.

During the summer, I like iced tea, root beer floats, and ice cream (sometimes frozen yogurt).

**15.06** | When a complete sentence lies entirely within parentheses at the end of a sentence, write the period inside the closing bracket.

Pres. Barack Obama signed the Affordable Care Act into law on March 23, 2010 (He was elected to the presidency in 2008.)

**15.07** | When an abbreviation ends with a period and falls within parentheses at the end of a sentence, no additional period is required.

✗ This happened two hundred years ago (i.e., 1816 A.D.).

☺ This happened two hundred years ago (i.e., 1816 A.D.)

**15.08** | If a sentence contains more than one parenthetic reference, the one at the end is placed before the period (but see Rule 15.06 and 15.07 for exceptions).

This sandstone (see fig. 6) is in every county of Ohio (see fig. 1).

**15.09** | The period is used sometimes in a series of three points to indicate an ellipsis. The points may be set with a space between each, or set flush with no spaces. The formatting is specific to the style guide you are using. See Chapter 10 for style rules on using the ellipsis.

Chicago Style (open ellipsis):

So . . . have you heard from James yet?

Chicago Style (closed ellipsis):

So...have you heard from James yet?

AP Style:

So ... have you heard from James yet?

**15.10** | The period is used in many abbreviations, but punctuation rules vary from one style guide to another. *Chicago Style* minimizes the use of periods in abbreviations, while *AP Style* calls for more liberal use, as the examples in the table below indicate. For rules on periods with specific abbreviations, refer to your particular style guide.

| Chicago | AP Style |
| --- | --- |
| PhD | Ph.D. |
| MA | M.A. |
| BA | B.A. |
| JD | J.D. |
| PO Box | P.O. Box |
| US | U.S. |
| UN | U.N. |

**15.11** | In computer terminology, the period is often called a "dot," and it is used in a number of ways, including in Website addresses, file names, and IP addresses, among others.

Facebook.com

Spectrum.org

document.txt

webpage.html

192.168.0.1

**15.12** | Do not use a period after single letters of the alphabet that represent names without specific designation.

Officer B, Subject A, Brand X, etc.

A said to B that all is well.

Mr. A told Mr. B that the case was closed.

Mr. X (for unknown or censored name)

but Mr. A. does not want to go

In this sentence, Mr. A. specifically refers to Mr. Andrews

**15.13** | A period can be used in place of a closing parenthesis after a letter or number that identifies an element in a list or series.

a. California

b. Oregon

c. Washington

1. apples

2. oranges

3. lemons

**15.14** | Use a period followed by a space after the middle initial in a person's name.

Daniel D. Tompkins, Ross T. McIntire

**15.15** | Do not use a period after Roman numerals written as ordinals.

King George V

Super Bowl XLII

Apollo XII

**15.16** | Use a period after a legend followed by descriptive language beneath a photo, diagram, or other illustration.

Figure 1. Image of Yellowstone Park

Figure 2. Bart and Betty on vacation in Wyoming.

If a legend stands alone with no descriptive language, omit the period.

Figure 1

Table 2

**15.17** | Use a period to separate integers from decimals in a single expression.

0.15 miles

$5.00

3.5 percent

3.65 meters

1.5 ounces

**15.18** | A period is sometimes used in place of a comma to indicate thousands in continental European languages.

3.1415

20.650.537

# Chapter 16
## Question Marks

The question mark, also called an interrogation point, signifies an interrogative clause or phrase. Simply put, it lets the reader known that a question is being asked. It is typically used at the end of a sentence in place of a full stop (period), but it can be used in other ways too, as noted below. We will begin this review of style rules governing the question mark with the most common example of how it is used.

**16.01** | Use a question mark at the end of a direct query to inform the reader that a question has been asked.

> Are you there?
>
> Where are my glasses?
>
> Elizabeth is missing; have you seen her?
>
> Will you ever grow up?

**16.02** | Use a question mark when a sentence is written in declarative form, but it is actually meant to be a question. The four examples below appear to be declarative clauses, but the question mark turns them into queries that require answers.

> You are, of course, familiar with New York?
>
> He really did it?
>
> That woman's name is Jessica?
>
> I should sign this contract now?

**16.03** | Use a full stop or an exclamation point instead of a question mark for an interrogative statement. At first glance, an interrogative statement appears to be a question; but it is a declaratory statement. If you write the closing punctuation as a question mark, it changes the sentence to a question. Just as vocal inflections tip off a listener to a speaker's intent, punctuation does the same with readers. As these examples show, the difference is subtle; but using the right punctuation can pack a powerful punch and enhance the quality of your writing.

Interrogative Statement:

How can you expect me to believe you!

☑ (expresses incredulity or indignation)

Query:

How can you expect me to believe you?

☑ (asks a question; an answer is expected)

Interrogative Statement:

Will you be shocked when I win the lotto!

☑ (expresses confidence or good fortune is imminent)

Query:

Will you be shocked when I win the lotto?

☑ (asks a question; an answer is expected)

Interrogative Statement:

Why can't I get any peace and quiet around here!

☑ (expresses frustration and, possibly, annoyance)

Query:

Why can't I get any peace and quiet around here?

☑ (asks a question; an answer is expected)

**16.04** | Use a period for an interrogative request—a sentence written in such a way that it appears to ask a question, but it is a request or a demand.

> Will you please forward my mail.

> Would you shut up and let me explain.

> Why can't I get any peace and quiet around here!

**16.05** | A question mark can be used parenthetically to indicate doubt. Not all style guides require parentheses around a question mark as shown in the following examples, but using them will help to eliminate confusion about the meaning. Either way, the punctuation is placed next to the word in question with no space preceding it.

> In 2016(?), David Colby met with an undercover agent in what turned out to be a videotaped sting operation.

> Leonardo da Vinci (1452?—1519)

> Donald met secretly with a woman named Melinda(?) and offered her fifty thousand cash to burn the incriminating photographs.

> The statue(?) was on the law books.

> ☑ (The writer is unsure of the spelling.)

> In 1934(?), Albert Szent-Györgyi discovered Vitamin C.

**16.06** | Use a question mark at the end of each interrogatory phrase in a series of such phrases cobbled together into a single sentence.

> Did he speak in a normal tone of voice? Or shout? Or whisper?

> Do you like dance music? Rock? Country? Classical? Jazz?

**16.07** | When several questions are asked together in the same sentence and have a common dependence, write a single question mark at the end of the series.

Where now are the friends I knew from the Eighties; the playful girls; the crazy DJs; the fun-loving bartenders; the great dance clubs where I used to hang out?

# Chapter 17
## Exclamation Points

The exclamation point (or exclamation mark in British English) is the mark used at the end of a word, phrase, or short sentence that expresses surprise or strong emotion (joy, anger, etc.) It has the same effect as a full stop. It dates back to the fifteenth century, when it was used with the Latin word "io," an exclamation of joy. Until the mid-seventeenth century, the exclamation point was called the "sign of admiration." In the 1950s, it was called the "bang," from comic strips that popularized interjections like "POW!" and "ZAP!" It did not have its own key on the standard typewriter keyboard until the 1970s; before then, it required typing a period, backspacing, and then typing an apostrophe.

Today, the exclamation point is widely used by writers in fiction and nonfiction, as well as in email, advertising, and other mediums. It is commonly used with exclamations like "Hi!" and "Wow!" as well as short phrases like "Well, that's great!" Profanity is usually followed by an exclamation point; for example, "Crap! I'm confused!"

Some writers of yesteryear expressed contempt for this mark. F. Scott Fitzgerald declared: "Cut out all these exclamation points...An exclamation point is like laughing at your own joke." But today, it is widely used. Recent studies have shown women use it more than men do, and in modern society, exclamation points function as markers of friendly interaction; for example, making "Hi!" or "Good luck!" seem friendlier than using a period in "Hi." or "Good luck."

There is no arguing that the exclamation point is here to stay, so it behooves the writer to learn the following rules for its proper use.

**17.01** | The exclamation point is used after an expression of great surprise or strong emotion, either positive (delight, pleasure, amazement) or negative (anger, shock, fear, outrage). The expression can be one syllable, a word, a short phrase, or a brief sentence.

"Look out!" he shouted.

He should be ashamed of himself!

What the heck!

How beautiful!

She groaned, "Oh my God!"

Mayday! Mayday!

**17.02** | Where an interjection is repeated without particular emphasis on one element in the series, each may be followed by a comma except the last.

Ha, ha, ha! That's very funny!

**17.03** | Avoid using an exclamation point with a compound sentence or with an overly long or complex sentence. If a detailed explanation is needed, rewrite the passage so that the details are separated from the interjection, and reduce the latter to a word or short phrase that expresses the requisite surprise or strong emotion.

✗ I received a call from a neighbor letting me know a robber had broken into my house; I hurried home and discovered that my computer and TV were gone, and I was so mad!

☺ I received a call from a neighbor letting me know a robber had broken into my house; I hurried home and discovered that my computer and TV were gone. I was so mad!

**17.04** | When the emotion is very strong, double exclamation points may be used:

Stop him!! That man is a murderer!!

**17.05** | When the word *oh* is used, the context determines whether an exclamation point is appropriate. If it is expressed as an acknowledgement, a desire, or an imprecation, as in the first two examples below, do not use an exclamation point. If it reflects surprise or strong emotion, as in the third example, then use it.

> Oh David, I just don't know what to say.

> Oh, yes. I knew about that.

> Oh! Really?

**17.06** | When the word *oh* is used in a sentence and the entire statement expresses surprise or strong emotion, write an exclamation point at the end of the sentence.

> Oh no, I can't believe you stole my car!

> Oh Lord, the ship is sinking!

> Oh, you are such an idiot!

**17.07** | Do not overuse the exclamation point. Generally, do not use it at all in writing nonfiction. It is meant to convey surprise or strong emotion. If you end too many sentences with exclamation points, they might lose their impact, and readers may perceive such overuse as unpolished, childish, or annoying.

# Chapter 18
## Dashes and Hyphens

**D**ashes and hyphens are commonly used as punctuation marks. Similar in appearance, they serve distinctly different purposes and confuse writers who are not familiar with their uses. The hyphen is a shorter mark; it typically links compound adjectives together and breaks long words that won't fit in the available space on a line. The dash is longer, and it is surprisingly useful. For instance, this dash—called an *em* dash—connects the parts of this sentence together into one statement to express a unified idea.

Used in pairs, dashes can set off short phrases within a sentence—like this example—eliminating the need for parentheses and extra commas. They are conspicuous in print and guide the reader's attention. You can use dashes to create sentences of varied complexity, adding interest and clarity to your writing style. But first, you must learn some basic style rules. Hyphen rules are discussed later in this chapter.

### Style Rules for Using the Dash

**18.01** | Most word processing software applications support the dash, but if yours does not, a double hyphen with no spaces in between may be substituted.

> The materials needed to build the dog house--lumber, plywood, and nails--should cost less than twenty dollars.

**18.02** | A dash can be used to convey an abrupt change in thought or construction.

> Allan tripped and fell—his wife was out shopping at the time.

We all agreed with the candidate—I still won't vote for him.

The taxi driver drove into the lake—he was drunk and should not have been driving.

**18.03** | A dash can be used to indicate sudden change in sentiment.

Many firefighters perished on 9/11—we honor their memory.

He brags that he is a billionaire—his wife knows it's not true.

Have you ever heard—but how could you possibly hear?

**18.04** | Use a dash to abruptly terminate a sentence. If you want the sentence to trail off, use an ellipsis instead.

Oh my God, I am so upset I could—

☑ The thought ends abruptly, so use a dash.

I was hoping you would call...

☑ The thought trails off, so use an ellipsis.

**18.05** | Use a dash at the end of an interrupted or an unfinished word.

Help! Someone is break—.

I deleted my profile on Face—.

**18.06** | A dash can be used to imply without expressing a conclusion.

He is a smart man but—

**18.07** | Dashes may be used in place of commas or parentheses to set off a short phrase that requires emphasis. Avoid overusing this construction, since dashes are conspicuous and too many can give a visual sense of choppy or stilted prose.

The weather is terrible—wind, rain, and fog—but we still have to drive home.

Three girls—Ellen, Connie, and Sue—are finalists in the beauty pageant.

**18.08** | A dash can be used at the end of a series of phrases that depend upon a concluding clause or where a final clause summarizes a series of ideas.

> Railroads and airplanes, factories and warehouses, wealth and luxury—these are not hallmarks of spirituality.

> Freedom of speech, freedom of worship, freedom of press—these are basic human rights promised by the U.S. Constitution.

**18.09** | A dash is used after an introductory phrase that leads into subsequent lines and indicates repetition of that phrase.

> I recommend—
>
>> That we submit them for review and corrections;
>>
>> That we then accept the corrections; and
>>
>> That we publish the corrected report.

**18.10** | A dash can be used to lead in to a phrase or expression added to an apparently complete sentence, but which refers back to some previous part of the sentence.

> He wondered what the candidate would say next—he had a habit of saying crazy things out of the blue.

**18.11** | Use a dash to mark pauses and repetitions for dramatic or rhetorical effect.

> They make a war and call it—peace.

> Life—is what you make it.

> You have published four novels—really?

> Sometimes I drink coffee—and sometimes tea.

**18.12** | When a word or expression is repeated for oratorical effect, a dash is used to introduce the repetition.

> Shakespeare was the greatest of all poets—Shakespeare, the great intellectual ocean whose waves washed the continents of all thought.

**18.13** | A phrase expressing strong or contrary actions or emotions can be set off from the surrounding sentence by a pair of dashes.

> She laughs—she cries—no matter what that man does, she loves him deeply.

**18.14** | You can use one or more dashes to set off repetition or different amplifications of the same statement.

> The madness of what he plans to do—the driving compulsion that he must do it—the dreadful horror of the act he is about to commit—the anger that burns in his soul—all these complicated factors have led the gun-toting man to the crime scene that he is about to create at this particular moment in time.

**18.15** | A dash can be used to indicate the unexpected or what is not the natural outcome of what has gone before:

> He walked along the sandy beach for hours looking for the perfect shell and found instead—trash.

**18.16** | A dash can be substituted in place of a conjunctive adverb such as *accordingly, namely, however,* etc.

> He excelled in three branches—math, chemistry, and physics.

> She promised to do the laundry—she wasn't in the mood and got drunk instead.

**18.17** | Use a dash to indicate one or more letters omitted from a word that you prefer not to write. This is commonly done with expletives.

> Gregory is an obnoxious jacka——. *(jackass)*

**18.18** | The dash is sometimes used in cataloging as a ditto mark.

> Allen, Tim. *Apocalypse Orphan.* Spectrum Ink, 2016
>
> —*Prisoners of the Game.* Spectrum Ink, 2016
>
> —*Return of Akavasha.* Spectrum Ink, 2016

**18.19** | A dash may be used to set off run-in questions and answers in court testimony and other similar transcripts.

Q. Did he go?—A. No.

**18.20** | To denote a gap of time, do not use a dash. Instead, use a hyphen between the two elements with no space on either side.

Monday-Friday

2016-2020

January-June

**18.21** | Use a dash between a citation and the authority.

"All the world's a stage."—Shakespeare

"Every man's work shall be made manifest."—I Corinthians 3:13

"Maybe everybody in the whole damn world is scared of each other."—John Steinbeck

**9.22** | The dash is used to precede a byline or a run-in credit byline, as shown at the bottom of the following four lines of verse, preceding the poet's name.

Lay the proud usurpers low!
Tyrants fall in every foe!
Liberty's in every blow!
Let us do or die!

—Robert Burns

**18.23** | Use a dash to define verse references in the Bible or page references in books. But if the dash is too conspicuous, a shorter, standard hyphen may be used. Either way, do not add a space before or after the dash or hyphen:

Matt. v: 1—11 or Matt. v: 1-11;

See pp. 50—53 or See pp. 50-53.

## Style Rules for Using the Hyphen

**18.50** | Use a hyphen to connect the elements of certain compound words, italicized in the following examples:

> A *man-eating* tiger chased me through the woods.

> He is a *hot-tempered* man.

> The girl works for a *family-owned* business.

> The employee *fast-tracked* himself into a management position.

**18.51** | Use a hyphen to indicate continuation of a word divided on a syllable at the end of a line (in a printed document or book). If you are unsure of where to put a hyphen in a long word, check your dictionary.

**18.52** | Use hyphens between the letters of a spelled-out word.

> The city where I live in California is spelled S-o-n-o-m-a.

> I'm a native of Halifax, so I am a H-a-l-i-g-o-n-i-a-n.

> The Iraqi militants took over F-a-l-l-u-j-a-h.

**18.53** | A hyphen is used to separate elements of chemical formulas.

> carbon-14

> 3-chloro-4-methylbenzoic acid

> F-actin

> Asp-His-Lys

> 2,4,6-tri-t-butylphenol

**18.54** | Use one or more hyphens to represent letters deleted from a word or illegible words in copy.

> Thousands died from the --bonic plague that swept through Europe in the Middle Ages.

> Gen. Colin Pow - - -

**18.55** | A hyphen can be used to set off numeric values, capital letters, and a mix of both.

Figures:

6-30-2016 (date)

1-703-765-6593 (telephone number)

230-20-8030 (Social Security number)

$15-$25 (range)

Capital Letters:

WTOP-AM-FM-TV (radio and television stations)

CBS-TV

AFL-CIO (union merger)

C-SPAN (satellite television)

Figures and Capitals:

6-A (exhibit identification)

DC-14 (airplane)

I-95 (interstate roadway)

MiG-25 (hyphen with letters and number value)

**18.56** | To denote a gap of time, do not use a dash. Instead, use a hyphen between the two elements with no space on either side.

Monday-Friday

2016-2020

January-June

**18.57** | Do not use a hyphen for the word "to" when that word precedes the first of two related figures or expressions.

✗ From June 1-July 30, 2005

☺ From June 1 to July 30, 2005

**18.58** | Do not use a hyphen for the word "and" when the word "between" precedes the first of two related figures or expressions.

✗ Between 2000-08

☺ Between 2000 and 2008

# Chapter 19
## Ellipses

The ellipsis is a punctuation mark that consists of three periods, or points. For example, this is an ellipsis . . . and it can be used in various ways. "Ellipsis" is a word from ancient Greek that means "falling short; omission." Common uses of this punctuation mark in present-day writing are to express: an unfinished thought; dialogue trailing off; a slight pause; an awkward silence; or a feeling of mystery. Some writers confuse the ellipsis with the dash, which indicates a more sudden interruption. The correct uses of the ellipsis are fairly straightforward and explained in the rules below.

**19.01** | An ellipsis consists of three points, either with a space between each point, or set flush with no spaces. The formatting varies from one style guide to another. If you opt to add spaces between the points, then you should use non-breaking spaces (an option available in most word processing applications) to prevent the points from breaking onto the next line. Also, depending on the style guide, you may be required to add a space before and after the ellipsis. If you use a closed ellipsis (the second example below) and adhere to *Chicago Manual of Style*, then the ellipsis is handled in the same manner as you would a dash.

Chicago Manual of Style (open ellipsis):

So . . . have you heard from James yet?

Chicago Manual of Style (closed ellipsis):

So...have you heard from James yet?

AP Style:

So ... have you heard from James yet?

In *Elements of Typographic Style,* Robert Bringhurst dismisses the open ellipsis as a "Victorian eccentricity. In most contexts, the [open] ellipsis is much too wide." He recommends using the closed ellipsis (three points, no spaces), or the prefabricated ellipsis character available in present-day word processing software, which is the preference of most writers. The examples given in the first two sections below are consistent with Chicago Style and generally appropriate for fiction writing.

**19.02** | Regardless of the ellipsis style you prefer, be consistent. Do not use an open ellipsis in one paragraph and switch to a closed ellipsis a few paragraphs later. Decide on a style and use it consistently from the first page to the last page of your project.

## Closed Ellipsis Rules

**19.10** | If a clause or phrase ends with an ellipsis, and it is a complete sentence that takes a question mark or exclamation point, put the ellipsis before the punctuation.

How did you...?

What in the world...?

**19.11** | If a clause ends with an ellipsis and it is a complete sentence, and if it should end with a period, you can write four dots (the three points of the ellipsis followed by a period); or the period can be omitted. Both of these examples are acceptable:

Now you've really done it....

Now you've really done it...

**19.12** | In a compound sentence connected by an ellipsis, you can sometimes omit the ending punctuation on the first clause and use only the ellipsis. Both of the sentences below are interrogatories, so we can connect them with the ellipsis and use one question mark at the end, as in the second example. Note that either construction is acceptable.

What the heck...? Who ate the ice cream?

What the heck...Who ate the ice cream?

**19.13** | If a phrase ends with an ellipsis and it is not a complete sentence, write only the ellipsis; no period (fourth point) is necessary.

✗ What the....

☺ What the...

**19.14** | If an ellipsis is used mid-stream in a sentence, and the phrase before it requires a comma or other punctuation, write the ellipsis after the punctuation, or omit the punctuation if you can do so without detracting from the clarity or flow of the sentence. Both of these examples are correct, but the second is the preferred construction:

**OK:** You can run,...but you cannot hide.

**Preferred:** You can run...but you cannot hide.

**19.15** | In dialogue, do not use a period, comma, or semicolon after an ellipsis. Treat the ellipsis as a full stop.

✗ "One day, the aliens will land and...," William whispered.

☺ "One day, the aliens will land and..." William whispered.

**19.16** | Two or more ellipses may be used in a sentence, and the same rules apply to both.

What I mean is...I just want to say...Oh, never mind.

**19.17** | When text is quoted from a printed source (book, newspaper, magazine, court transcript, etc.) or from a digital source such as a website, use an ellipsis to denote words that have been omitted to save space or for brevity.

Britain voted to leave the European Union...Electoral officials announced that the "Leave" campaign had racked up 17.4 million votes, compared to 16.1 million backing the status quo...The result sent shock waves through global financial markets.

**19.18** | When text is quoted as described in Rule 19.17, an ellipsis is usually not placed before the first word or after the last word of the quoted text unless the writer intends for the sentence to be incomplete.

## Open Ellipsis Rules

The following examples and rules are the same as the *Closed Ellipses Rules* given above and are repeated here to show the differences in how open ellipses should be written.

**19.20** | If a clause or phrase ends with an ellipsis, and it is a complete sentence that takes a question mark or exclamation point, put the ellipsis before the punctuation.

How did you . . . ?

What in the world . . . ?

**19.21** | If a clause ends with an ellipsis and it is a complete sentence, and if it should end with a period, you can write four dots (the three points of the ellipsis followed by a period); or the period can be omitted. Both of these examples are acceptable:

Now you've really done it . . . .

Now you've really done it . . .

**19.22** | In a compound sentence connected by an ellipsis, you can sometimes omit the ending punctuation on the first clause and use only the ellipsis. Both of the sentences below are interrogatories, so we can connect them with the ellipsis and use one question mark at the end, as in the second example. Note that either construction is acceptable.

What the heck . . . ? Who ate the ice cream?

What the heck . . . Who ate the ice cream?

**19.23** | If a phrase ends with an ellipsis and it is not a complete sentence, write only the ellipsis; no period (fourth point) is necessary.

✗ What the . . . .

☺ What the . . .

**19.24** | If an ellipsis is used mid-stream in a sentence, and the phrase before it requires a comma or other punctuation, write the ellipsis after the punctuation, or omit the punctuation if you can do so without detracting from the clarity or flow of the sentence. Both of these examples are correct, but the second is the preferred construction:

You can run, . . . but you cannot hide.

You can run . . . but you cannot hide.

**19.25** | In dialogue, do not use a period, comma, or semicolon after an ellipsis. Treat the ellipsis as a full stop.

✗ "One day, the aliens will land and . . . ," William whispered.

☺ "One day, the aliens will land and . . ." William whispered.

**19.26** | Two or more ellipses may be used in a sentence, and the same rules apply to both.

What I mean is . . . I just want to say . . . Oh, never mind.

**19.27** | When text is quoted from a printed source (book, newspaper, magazine, court transcript, etc.) or from a digital source such as a website, use an ellipsis to denote words that have been omitted to save space or for brevity.

Britain voted to leave the European Union . . . Electoral officials announced that the "Leave" campaign had racked up 17.4 million votes, compared to 16.1 million backing the status quo . . . The result sent shock waves through global financial markets.

**19.28** | When text is quoted as described in Rule 19.27, an ellipsis is usually not placed before the first word or after the last word of the quoted text unless the writer intends for the sentence to be incomplete.

## AP Style Ellipsis Rules

The following examples are the same as the *Closed* and *Open Ellipses Rules* given previously and are repeated here to illustrate the differences in how ellipses should be written in AP Style.

**19.30** | If a clause or phrase ends with an ellipsis, and it is a complete sentence that takes a question mark or exclamation point, put the ellipsis before the punctuation.

> How did you ... ?

> What in the world ... ?

**19.31** | If a clause ends with an ellipsis and it is a complete sentence, and if it should end with a period, you can write four dots (the three points of the ellipsis followed by a period); or the period can be omitted. Both of these examples are acceptable:

> Now you've really done it ... .

> Now you've really done it ...

**19.32** | In a compound sentence connected by an ellipsis, you can sometimes omit the ending punctuation on the first clause and use only the ellipsis. Both of the sentences below are interrogatories, so we can connect them with the ellipsis and use one question mark at the end, as in the second example. Note that either construction is acceptable.

> What the heck ... ? Who ate the ice cream?

> What the heck ... Who ate the ice cream?

**19.33** | If a phrase ends with an ellipsis and it is not a complete sentence, write only the ellipsis; no period (fourth point) is necessary.

> ✗ What the ... .

> ☺ What the ...

**19.34** | If an ellipsis is used mid-stream in a sentence, and the phrase before it requires a comma or other punctuation, write the ellipsis after the punctuation, or omit the punctuation if you can do so without detracting from the clarity or flow of the sentence. Both of these examples are correct, but the second is the preferred construction:

> You can run, . . . but you cannot hide.

> You can run . . . but you cannot hide.

**19.35** | In dialogue, do not use a period, comma, or semicolon after an ellipsis. Treat the ellipsis as a full stop.

> ✗ "One day, the aliens will land and ... ," William whispered.

> ☺ "One day, the aliens will land and ..." William whispered.

**19.36** | Two or more ellipses may be used in a sentence, and the same rules apply to both.

> What I mean is ... I just want to say ... Oh, never mind.

**19.37** | When text is quoted from a printed source (book, newspaper, magazine, court transcript, etc.) or from a digital source such as a website, use an ellipsis to denote words that have been omitted to save space or for brevity.

> Britain voted to leave the European Union ... Electoral officials announced that the "Leave" campaign had racked up 17.4 million votes, compared to 16.1 million backing the status quo ... The result sent shock waves through global financial markets.

**19.38** | When text is quoted as described in Rule 19.37, an ellipsis is usually not placed before the first word or after the last word of the quoted text unless the writer intends for the sentence to be incomplete.

# Chapter 20
## Quotation Marks

Quotation marks are used to set off the exact words spoken by others. Also called quotes, quote marks, and inverted commas, this symbol was developed by French printers in the 1500s. At first, only a single quotation mark was used, and it was placed in the outside margin of a page to call attention to an important passage, not just a quotation. By the mid-sixteenth century, its appearance had changed to the double inverted comma that we use today. In the seventeenth century, printers began employing this punctuation mark in pairs to set off quotations. The single quotation mark surfaced in the early 1800s as a way to indicate a nested quote within a quote.

In addition to setting off direct quotations, these marks have other uses. Quote marks can be used to emphasize a word or phrase, and to set off titles of books, movies, and other creative works. The style rules given in this chapter will acquaint writers with the various ways in which quotation marks are employed in modern writing.

**20.01** | Every direct quotation in a sentence must be enclosed within quotation marks.

> "The night sky is beautiful," she said with a dreamy smile.

> He shouted, "Watch out!"

**20.02** | Each part of an interrupted quotation in a sentence must begin and end with quotation marks.

"I believe," the detective declared, "that the suspect killed his neighbor."

The stranger warned, "Whatever you do, don't drink the water!"

**20.03** | Titles of books, articles, poems, and certain other works are often enclosed in quotation marks (although some style guides state that such titles should be italicized). The rules for capitalizing and formatting titles can be confusing and are discussed at length in Chapter 23 on capitalization and Chapter 24 on titles.

**20.04** | Reports of what another person has said in words other than his own are called *indirect quotations* and take no quote marks.

He said he would go if he could.

✍ This is an indirect quotation, so don't use quote marks.

He said, "I would go if I could."

✍ This is a direct quotation, so use quote marks.

**20.05** | In a direct quotation that spans multiple paragraphs, place an opening quote mark at the beginning of each paragraph, and place a closing quote mark only at the end of the last paragraph.

"This is paragraph 1.

"This is paragraph 2.

"This is paragraph 3."

✍ Notice the closing quotation mark at the end of Paragraph 3.

**20.06** | A *secondary quotation*, or a direct quotation nested within another quotation, must be enclosed in single quote marks. In the sentence below, *Put down that gun!* is a secondary quotation.

He said: "I heard her cry, 'He has a gun!' and then I heard a shot."

**20.07** | Limit quotation marks to three sets (double, single, double). If a sentence contains more than three sets of quotation marks, rewrite it to avoid this awkward construction.

> The policeman said: "We received a call from an anonymous caller who reported, 'A man dressed in military fatigues yelled, "Die, you scum!" and then he denoted a bomb and blew up the restaurant.'"

**20.08** | When a quotation ends a sentence, place the period before the closing quote mark.

> Jill said, "Please hand me the salt."

Note that periods and other punctuation marks in sentences ending with a direct quotation may follow different rules in British English. Consult *Oxford Style Guide* for details.

**20.09** | When a quotation ends with a comma, place the closing quote mark after the comma.

> "I enjoy reading science-fiction novels," Calvin said.

**20.10** | When a quotation ends with punctuation other than a period or a comma, write the punctuation inside the quote marks only if it is part of the matter quoted.

> "Ellen," muttered Bob in a low voice, "you are a liar."

> Who came up with the saying "Drop the gun"?

> Who asked "Why?"

> Why call it a "gentlemen's agreement"?

**20.11** | Use quotation marks to enclose any matter following such terms as *entitled, the word, the term, marked, named, cited as, referred to as,* or *signed*; but do not use quotation marks to enclose expressions that follow the terms *known as, called, so-called,* etc., unless such expressions are misnomers or slang.

> Be sure to spell the word "caricature" correctly.

> The term "medical malpractice" does not apply in this case.

> The letter was signed "John Quincy Smith."

> The man known as The Zodiac Killer has never been caught.

> He didn't like any of the so-called candidates.

**20.12** | When information is enclosed within quotation marks and the reader must understand that the punctuation is not part of the quoted matter, the symbol can be placed outside of the closing quotation mark. For example, in a tutorial on using Microsoft Windows™, it may be necessary to tell the reader to type a command, and placing the period outside of the closing quotation mark makes it clear that the mark itself should not be typed.

> Open a command prompt and type "regedit".

> On page 10, at the end of the first sentence, insert the word "maintenance".

> Change "February 1, 2016" to "May 30, 2016".

**20.13** | When a quotation is lengthy (i.e., more than a short sentence) or introduced in a formal manner, it is usually preceded by a colon.

> He declared: "The stock market is unpredictable, driven by world events beyond the control of investors. There are no guarantees that a stock or bond investment will be profitable."

**20.14** | Use quotation marks to set off misnomers, slang expressions, coined words, and words or phrases used in a notable, ironic, or unusual manner.

> It was a "gentlemen's agreement."

> The "invisible government" is responsible.

> Her "beautiful smile" is as fake as a three-dollar bill.

George Herman "Babe" Ruth.

After the word "treaty," insert a comma.

The check was endorsed "John Adamson."

The postcard was signed "John."

**20.15** | Quotation marks are not used in poetry, except to set off dialogue spoken in the poem. The lines of a poem should align on the left, those that rhyme taking the same indention.

Why seek to scale Mount Everest,

Queen of the air?

Why strive to crown that cruel crest

And deathward dare?

Said Mallory of dauntless quest:

"Because it's there."

**20.16** | Sentences from a foreign language are usually enclosed in quotation marks. Single foreign words should be written in italics. But if a foreign word is widely used and the writer believes it is familiar to most readers, it need not be italicized.

**20.17** | When a quoted word or phrase appears at the end of a sentence and the quoted matter is followed by a footnote, place the footnote reference after the closing quote mark.

The politician claimed the award was "unjustified."[1]

Kelly's words were: "The facts in the case prove otherwise."[2]

**20.18** | Avoid overuse of quotation marks. Familiar expressions, clichés, and sayings that most readers have heard numerous times before need not be quoted. Lists of words presented merely as words, and lists of books, plays, movies, or songs, should be printed without quotation marks. Excessive use of quote marks can spoil the look of the page and make the content difficult to read.

# Chapter 21
## Apostrophes and Possessives

The apostrophe is a punctuation mark that has varied uses in the English language. It can form the possessive case for singular and plural nouns, noun phrases, and pronouns (the man's book, Robert's wife, the cars' buyers). It can denote omitted letters, as with contractions (don't, can't, wouldn't). The apostrophe can form certain plural nouns, such as single letters and digits (I count three 4's and six b's on that page; Be sure to dot your i's); and it has several other uses.

The first known use of the apostrophe dates back to the 1490s in France. The symbol soon found its way into English literature, where it often stood for a missing letter or a contraction. Its use evolved over time, and by the eighteenth century, rules for writing possessives and plurals were widely followed in Europe. The present-day apostrophe has the appearance of a closing single quotation mark, although the symbols are used in a different manner.

Many writers dismiss apostrophes as elementary and easy to figure out. But this mark is more versatile than meets the eyes and has more than two dozen rules and exceptions. Some rules are fairly complex, leading to frequent punctuation errors. In some cases, a misplaced or incorrectly used apostrophe can change the meaning of a sentence to something other than what the writer intended.

The rules for possessive apostrophes and plural possessives, in particular, tend to be a source of confusion for writers. The fact that rules vary from one style guide to another adds to the confusion. For our purposes, we will look to *Chicago Manual of Style* as our authority.

If you are using another guide such as *AP Style* or *APA Style*, consult the applicable sections for the rules pertaining to apostrophes.

**21.01** | For singular and plural common nouns not ending in *s*, form the possessive case by adding an apostrophe and an *s*.

<u>Singular nouns:</u>

>the pastor's sermon

>the chef's salad

>a boy's bicycle

>his car's tires

<u>Plural nouns:</u>

>the men's suits

>the women's fashion department

>the children's toys

>the people's choice

**21.02** | For singular common nouns ending in *s*, form the possessive case by adding an apostrophe and an *s*.

>The witness's testimony was not credible.

>My boss's car was stolen.

>The bus's tire blew out on the freeway.

Some writers may be accustomed to adding an apostrophe and omitting the possessive *s* after common nouns that end in *s* (for example, *Bernie Sanders' speech*). In Chicago Style, this practice is antiquated and the above rule should be followed.

**21.03** | For plural common nouns ending in *s*, form the possessive case by adding an apostrophe.

>the four kittens' mother

>the students' questions

>The three moms' kids were well-behaved.

**21.04** | For nouns plural in form (ending in *s*) but that have singular meaning, add an apostrophe to form the possessive case.

> Shingles' symptoms can be quite painful.

> the European countries' trade agreement

> the X-*Files* series' actors

**21.05** | For proper nouns ending in *s*, to form the possessive case, add an apostrophe + *s* if singular; or use only an apostrophe if the proper noun is plural.

> Bernie Sanders's speech

> Bill Gates's foundation

> the Obamas' family portrait

> the writers' short stories

**21.06** | For common nouns, and for proper nouns that end in an unpronounced *s*, form the possessive case by adding an apostrophe + *s*.

> Arkansas's northern border is Missouri's southern border.

> Descartes's writings are the foundation of Western philosophy.

**21.07** | For singular common nouns ending in *s* and followed by a word that begins with *s*, add an apostrophe to form the possessive case.

> For goodness' sake, please stop!

> for old times' sake

> The witness' story was not credible.

**21.08** | For singular common nouns that end with an *s* sound but not the letter *s*, add an apostrophe + *s* to form the possessive case.

> For appearance's sake, wear a shirt and tie.

> Science's 2015 breakthrough was a genome-editing technique.

> She should tell her husband for her conscience's sake.

It is often preferable to rewrite a sentence to avoid clumsy syntax and improve the flow. Following are the two above sentences restyled:

> For the sake of appearance, wear a shirt and tie.

> She should tell her husband for the sake of her conscience.

**21.09** | For compound nouns, form the possessive case by adding an apostrophe + *s* to the element nearest the object possessed.

> The reaction to the attorney general's decision was predictable.

> The lawnmower blade's edge was razor sharp.

**21.10** | Joint possession is indicated by placing an apostrophe on the last element of a series. Individual or alternative possession requires the use of an apostrophe on each element in a series.

> Paul and Linda's racy novel raised eyebrows.

> ☑ Paul and Linda are writing a novel together, so use one apostrophe on the last element.

> Paul's and Linda's novels may become bestsellers.

> ☑ Paul and Linda are each writing a separate novel, so use apostrophes on both names to show individual possession.

**21.11** | Generally, do not use an apostrophe after the names of countries or organized bodies ending in the letter *s*. Otherwise, use an apostrophe and add *s*.

> United States influence

> United Nations meeting

> Massachusetts laws

> House of Representatives session

> Teamsters Union

> Russia's oil exports

> Senate's rules of order

**21.12** | Possessive pronouns do not take an apostrophe—only nouns can have a possessive case that requires an apostrophe. The possessive pronouns are: *hers, his, ours, yours, theirs,* and *its.*

Remember: *its* is a possessive pronoun; *it's* is an abbreviation for *it is.*

**21.13** | An apostrophe generally is not used after words more descriptive than possessive (does not indicate personal possession), except when a plural does not end in *s.*

<u>Nouns more descriptive than possessive:</u>

>Proofreaders Guidelines
>
>Writers Workshop

<u>Nouns more descriptive than possessive but do not end in s:</u>

>children's hospital
>
>women's shoes

**21.14** | Possessive indefinite and impersonal pronouns require an apostrophe.

>Why is *someone's* footprint outside my window?
>
>It is said that one's eyes are a reflection of the soul.
>
>The authors signed *each other's* books.
>
>That was *another's* idea.
>
>They dressed in some *others'* clothing.

**21.15** | Use an apostrophe to indicate omission of letters in dialect, in contractions, and in poetry.

>I'm = I am
>
>who's = who is
>
>didn't = did not
>
>could've = could have

That's 'ow 'tis. = That's how it is.

'Twas so easy. = It was so easy.

aren't = are not

d'you = do you

should've = should have [**not** *should of*!]

**21.16** | The singular possessive case is used in general terms such as the following:

| | |
|---|---|
| arm's length | attorney's fees |
| baker's dozen | editor's revisions |
| printer's ink | confectioner's sugar |
| buyer's remorse | cow's milk |
| writer's cramp | doctor's advice |

**21.17** | Four-digit year dates can be abbreviated by substituting an apostrophe for the first two digits, although the practice is frowned upon because it creates ambiguity.

The summer of '65

Obama was re-elected in '12.

The Spirit of '76

**21.18** | Use the apostrophe to form the plural of letters and digits.

Cross your t's and dot your i's.

Computers run binary code made up of a series of 0's and 1's.

This sentence contains seven E's and no 2's.

**21.19** | While an apostrophe is used to indicate possession and contractions, it is not necessary as a rule to use an apostrophe to show the plural form of most initials, acronyms, and abbreviations, except where it is required for the sake of clarity.

49ers

FAQs

ABCs

1920s

IOUs, IPOs, SUVs

during the twenties

2-by-4s (or two-by-fours)

IQs

in her 70s (better: in her seventies)

during the '20s (better: during the 1920s)

Watch your p's and q's.

He never crosses his t's.

Way too many S's in this chapter!

**21.20** | When the plural form of an acronym is shown in parentheses, include a lowercase *s* within the parentheses.

(IPOs)

(MP3s)

(SUVs)

(JPEGs)

**21.21** | Omit the apostrophe in the shortened forms of most commonly used words.

Halloween, not Hallowe'en

possum, not 'possum

But *ma'am* requires an apostrophe, and so does *o'clock*.

**21.22** | The plural of spelled-out numbers, words referred to as words, and words containing an apostrophe is formed by adding *s* or *es*. But an apostrophe + *s* is added to indicate the plural of words used as words if omitting the apostrophe would make the passage difficult to read.

> twos, threes, sevens
>
> yeses and noes
>
> ands, ifs, and buts
>
> yeas and nays
>
> ins and outs
>
> the haves and have-nots
>
> ups and downs
>
> do's and don'ts

**21.23** | The possessive case is often used in lieu of an objective phrase, even though direct ownership is not involved.

> one day's labor
>
> four weeks' pay
>
> 12 days' labor
>
> 12 hours' travel time
>
> for charity's sake
>
> a stone's throw
>
> one dollar's worth
>
> five dollars' worth
>
> but $200 million worth

**21.24** | A possessive noun used in an adjective sense requires the addition of an apostrophe + *s*.

> He is a friend of John's.
>
> Betty's is the white house on the corner.

**21.25** | A noun that precedes a gerund should be written in the possessive case. A *gerund* is a word derived from a verb but that serves as a noun and ends in *-ing*. In the two examples that follow, the gerunds are italicized, and the possessive nouns are italicized and underlined.

We expected *Alice's meddling*, so no one was surprised.

*Jason's whining* irritated everyone at the party.

# Chapter 22
## Parentheses and Brackets

**P**arentheses allow you to introduce into a sentence a phrase that is not directly connected to the main statement but helps to make it clear. Normally used in pairs, parentheses tend to be ignored by present-day writers in favor of the dash, especially in fiction. But this punctuation mark has legitimate uses and should not be overlooked by those wanting to add variety and interest to their writing style.

Brackets, discussed later in this chapter, are often confused with parentheses. They are normally written in pairs but serve distinctly different purposes and should not be used where parentheses are clearly indicated. The rules given below explain when and how to correctly use parentheses and brackets correctly in your writing.

**22.01** | Parentheses may be used to introduce into a sentence a phrase that is not essentially connected to the main statement but helps make it clear. A parenthetic phrase must be enclosed in a pair of parentheses.

> Expulsion was inevitable when the student (who was on academic probation) was caught cheating on his math exam.

> This year (1914) saw the outbreak of a war that engulfed Europe.

> The result (see fig. 2) is most unexpected.

> China is the main buyer (by value) of oil exports from Iran (23 percent in 2014 and 19 percent in 2015).

**2.02** | When the unity of a sentence is broken or a parenthetic phrase disrupts the flow of a sentence too much to be set off by commas, the words causing the break should be enclosed in parentheses.

> The red Ford SUV was speeding (I witnessed it personally) less than two minutes before it crashed into a utility pole.

**22.03** | Use parentheses to enclose an explanatory word that is not part of a written statement if doing so eliminates confusion or enhances the clarity of the sentence.

> I subscribe to the Santa Barbara (CA) News-Press
>
> (but spell out News-Press of Santa Barbara, California)

**22.04** | Parentheses can be used to enclose letters or numbers designating items in a series, either at the beginning of paragraphs or within a paragraph.

> The building materials will be delivered in this order: (1) lumber, (2) drywall, (3) insulation, and (4) nails, screws, and tape.
>
> You will observe that the kerosene lantern is (a) an antique, (b) works well, and (3) the glass globe is very clear for its age.
>
> Paragraph 4(C)(2)(a) will be found on page 9.

**22.05** | Parentheses can be used, in pairs or singly, to enclose letters or numbers that mark division and classification in arguments or precise statements. These lists may be presented in several ways:

> (a) a) (1) 1)

**22.06** | Use parentheses to enclose a number inserted to confirm a written value that is spelled out, as in the below example. This is common practice in contracts, legal documents, and business correspondence.

> This job must be completed in sixty (60) days.
>
> Employees are entitled to three (3) weeks of paid vacation after one (1) year of full-time employment.

**22.07** | When an abbreviation ends with a period and falls within parentheses at the end of a sentence, no additional period is required.

✗ This happened two hundred years ago (i.e., 1816 A.D.).

☺ This happened two hundred years ago (i.e., 1816 A.D.)

**22.08** | A parenthetic reference at the end of a sentence is placed before the period, unless it is a complete sentence in itself; in that case, place the period inside the closing parenthesis.

During the summer, I like iced tea, sodas, and ice cream (sometimes frozen yogurt).

✏ The phrase sometimes frozen yogurt is not a complete sentence, so the period goes after the closing parenthesis.

President Obama signed the Affordable Care Act into law in 2010 (He was elected in 2008.)

✏ This parenthetical reference is a complete sentence that stands on its own, so the period goes inside the closing parenthesis.

**22.09** | If a sentence contains more than one parenthetic reference, place the period outside the closing parenthesis of the last reference.

This species of tree (see fig. 6) is found growing in every county of Oregon (see fig. 1).

**22.10** | When a number is followed by a letter in parentheses, no space is used between the number and the opening parenthesis. But if the letter is not in parentheses and the number is repeated with each letter, write the letter after the number with no space between.

15(a). Nails, bolts, and screws

15a. Nails, bolts, and screws

**22.11** | When content in parentheses spans more than one paragraph, start each paragraph with an opening parenthesis, and write the closing parenthesis at the end of the last paragraph.

(This is paragraph 1.

(This is paragraph 2.

(This is paragraph 3.)

Notice the closing parenthesis after Paragraph 3.

**22.12** | Parentheses are used in reports of speeches to set off the name of the person who is being referenced, and to indicate expressions on the part of the audience.

The honorable gentleman who introduced this legislation (Mr. Smith) knows more about international law than anyone on this floor. (Applause)

**22.13** | Question marks and exclamation points enclosed within parentheses can be used to show doubt about a statement or to express surprise or sarcasm. In fiction writing, this is rarely done and therefore should be avoided.

He said that on January 5th (?), he was in New York.

He is a most amazing (!) man.

**22.14** | Use parentheses to enclose remarks apparently made by the writer of the text. Note that brackets enclose remarks made by the editor or reviewer of that text.

The employer's policy on overtime wages was amended on March 2, 2016 (I fact-checked this myself).

The employer's policy on overtime wages was amended on March 2, 2016. (I fact-checked this myself.) [Joe, this doesn't seem right; recheck your facts.]

## Rules for Writing Brackets

**22.30** | Use brackets to enclose words or phrases which are entirely independent of the rest of the sentence. The enclosed words are usually comments, queries, corrections, criticisms, or directions inserted by some person other than the original writer or speaker.

**22.31** | Brackets are used in court transcripts, government hearings, some legal documents, and other records to enclose interpolations which are not part of the original quotation, such as a correction, explanation, omission, editorial comment, or a notation that a particular error is reproduced literally.

Our conference [lasted] two hours.

The statue [sic] was on the law books.

The general [MacArthur] ordered him to leave.

The paper was as follows [reads]:

I do not know. [Continues reading:]

They fooled only themselves. [Laughter]

The Witness: He did it that way [indicating].

Q. Do you know these men? [Hands a list to the witness]

The bill had *not* been paid [emphasis added].

Witness: This matter is classified. [Deleted]

Mr. Jones: Please hold up your hands. [Show of hands]

Q. [Continuing]

A. [Interrupting]

[Discussion off the record]

Witness [interrupting]: It is known—

Mr. Jones [continuing]: Now let us take the next item.

Mr. Smith [presiding]: Do you mean that literally?

The Chairman [to Mr. Smith]:

[Mr. Smith makes a further statement off the record.]

Mr. Jones [for Mr. Smith]:

Speak up. [A voice from the audience]

Be quiet! [Several voices from the audience]

**22.32** | Brackets are used to enclose passages of doubtful authenticity in reprints of early manuscripts, amendments to legislative bills, legal documents, and other portions of a text which that should be flagged as questionable.

**22.33** | Brackets are used in legal and ecclesiastical papers to indicate numerical words that may have to be changed, or to indicate where details are to be supplied.

This is the first [*second or third*] publication.

The board members shall remain in office until [*state date*] or until their successors are trained and fully qualified.

**22.34** | Brackets are used to avoid the confusion that would otherwise be caused by a parenthesis nested within a parenthesis.

On hot summer days, I like iced tea, lemonade, and ice cream (sometimes frozen [or merely refrigerated] yogurt).

**22.35** | Brackets are used in bills, contracts, laws, etc., to indicate matter that is to be omitted.

**22.36** | Brackets are used in various ways in mathematics.

$[5 + 4 \times (5 + 6)]/7$

$[10 ,6] = \text{LCM}(10,6) = 30$

**22.37** | When content in brackets spans more than one paragraph, start each paragraph with a bracket, and write the closing bracket at the end of the last paragraph.

[This is paragraph 1.

[This is paragraph 2.

[This is paragraph 3.]

Notice the closing bracket after Paragraph .

# PART III
# CAPITALIZATION RULES

# Chapter 23
## Capitalization Made Easy

Capital letters emphasize certain words to distinguish them from the surrounding text. The rules for capitalization in English grammar are reasonably straightforward and must be followed to produce a polished final draft of your manuscript. Some writers go overboard capitalizing many words that should be written in lowercase; or they overlook proper nouns that should be capitalized. Either way, such errors create an unfavorable impression that may invite rejection letters when you submit your project to an agent or publisher, or negative reviews and disappointing sales if you self-publish. Follow these basic rules of capitalization to self-edit your manuscript and produce a final draft you can submit or self-publish with pride and confidence.

**23.01** | Capitalize the first word of every complete sentence.

> Life is what you make it.
>
> The Internet has revolutionized the world.
>
> I think...therefore I am.
>
> Oh my God, I won the lottery!

**23.02** | Capitalize the first word of a sentence even if that word is a trademark, acronym, or proper noun not usually capitalized. Notice how the trademarked names *iPhone* and eBay are handled in these examples:

> IPhone users may buy iPhone accessories from the iStore.
>
> EBay is a popular site. He bought his iPad on eBay.

**23.03** | Capitalize proper nouns, including the names of people, places, and holidays.

| | | |
|---|---|---|
| David Smith | Caesar | Easter |
| England | Golden Gate Bridge | Pacific Ocean |
| Paris, France | Queen Elizabeth | San Francisco |

**23.04** | Capitalize the first word in every direct question.

Let me ask you; "How old are you?"

Who are you? Are you the detective Donald hired?

"Where are my car keys?" Carole asked.

**23.05** | Capitalize a one-word interjection or interrogatory when it stands alone.

Oh! I completely forgot to call you.

Really?

Facebook has blocked my account. Argh!

Ah! I pity that man.

**23.06** | Capitalize the first word of a sentence fragment, and capitalize any single word that stands alone in running copy.

What the heck...

Yes! Really! I thought you knew...

Umm...

Days turning to weeks, months to years...

**23.07** | Capitalize the first word of every quotation.

Mark demanded, "Stop the car! Now!"

"Why do you want to know?" Naomi asked with a frown.

"I apologized," Jackson said, "but you wouldn't accept it."

**23.08** | For all titles, capitalize the first word and the last word of the title. Capitalize all nouns, pronouns, adjectives, verbs, adverbs, and subordinating conjunctions. Capitalize prepositions only if they are used adverbially or adjectivally; otherwise, lowercase prepositions. Lowercase articles (*a, an, the*), coordinating conjunctions, and the word "to" in an infinitive, such as "How to Play the Violin." See also the full set of rules on writing and formatting titles in Chapter 15.

> *The Lord of the Rings*, a book by J. R. R. Tolkien, and a movie
>
> *Apocalypse Orphan*, a science-fiction novel by Tim Allen
>
> *The Creation of Adam*, a masterpiece by Michelangelo

**23.09** | Capitalize the first word in every line of a poem.

> If you can keep your head when all about you
> Are losing theirs and blaming it on you,
> If you can trust yourself when all men doubt you,
> But make allowance for their doubting too;
> If you can wait and not be tired by waiting,
> Or being lied about, don't deal in lies,
> Or being hated, don't give way to hating,
> And yet don't look too good, nor talk too wise...
>
> —excerpt from Rudyard Kipling's *If*

**23.10** | Trademarks and service marks are proper nouns and should be capitalized. Product names officially spelled with a lowercase letter, such as iPhone, are exceptions and should be lowercased, but see Rule 23.02 for an exception. Include the required legal symbol after the mark with no space between. The following symbols are acceptable: ™, (tm), (TM), and SM, (sm), (SM). Note that ™ and SM are preferred, but all the examples below are correct. Rules on using trademarks and generic product names in your writing are given in Chapter 9.

| | |
|---|---|
| Kleenex™ | Band-Aid(tm) |
| Clorox(TM) | WalmartSM |
| Citicorp(sm) | Yahoo!(SM) |

**23.11** | Capitalize the days of the week, the months of the year, and capitalize both the day and month when they appear together in a date.

Monday, Tuesday, Wednesday, etc.

January, February, March, etc.

The meeting was scheduled for 2 p.m. on Friday, March 17.

**23.12** | Capitalize words derived from proper names.

| | |
|---|---|
| American | Irish |
| Christian | Islamic |
| Martian | Mercurial |

**23.13** | Capitalize the first word of every numbered clause, regardless of how the clauses are structured in the paragraph.

The witness asserts: (1) That he saw the man attacked; (2) That he saw him fall; (3) That he saw the defendant flee.

The defendant claims that:

(1) He did not attack the man;

(2) The witness appeared drunk at the time;

(3) In fact, the witness himself attacked the man.

**23.14** | Capitalize Roman numerals when they are part of a proper name, a title, or a chapter heading.

| | |
|---|---|
| World War II | Pope John Paul II |
| Elizabeth II | Section III |
| Chapter V | Plate X |
| Figure IX | Book II |

**23.15** | Do not capitalize words such as river, mountain, sea, etc., when used as common nouns. But when used with an adjective or adjunct to specify a particular location, they become proper names and should be capitalized.

| | |
|---|---|
| Mississippi River | the overflowing river |
| Mediterranean Sea | the towering mountains |
| Alleghany Mountains | the ocean waves |
| Arctic Ocean | Sea of Galilee |

**23.16** | The cardinal points (north, south, east, and west) are common nouns and not capitalized. But when used to distinguish a particular location or region, they become proper nouns and should be capitalized.

The North fought against the South.

I will be traveling in the West.

The West Coast

The Middle East

The Midwest (U.S.)

If you go west in California, you will reach the ocean.

I have never been to western Europe.

**23.17** | Capitalize the names of political parties, religious denominations, and schools of thought.

| | | |
|---|---|---|
| Democrat | Republican | Quaker |
| Catholic | Presbyterian | Methodist |
| Buddhist | Freemason | Wiccan |

**23.18** | Do not capitalize the names of the four seasons unless the name is used as a proper noun or in a title or headline.

The summer was hot, the fall breezy, and the winter brutally cold.

The Winter of My Discontent

Will you be taking summer classes?

Cindy enjoys baking pies and cakes in the winter.

The Monterey Summer Festival

✍️ This is a specific event, and a proper noun, so capitalize.

I plan to attend three summer music festivals.

✍️ These festivals are generic, so use lowercase.

Then Winter—with her virgin snow—settled over the town.

✍️ Wait! Why is "Winter" capitalized? See Rule 23.19 below.

**23.19** | Personification is a concept in which inanimate objects are represented as having life and action. A personified noun is a proper noun and must be capitalized.

Clear-eyed Day broke on the horizon.

The Redwood said to the Oak, "I am taller than you."

The starry Night shook the dew from her wings.

Then Winter—with her virgin snow—settled over the town.

**23.20** | Capitalize a title when it precedes a person's name. When the title follows the name, it is a common noun, so write it lowercase.

Barack Obama, president of the United States, toured the city.

The mayor gave President Obama a tour of the flooded city.

The president of the United States attended the summit in Berlin.

Chairman Mark Murphy adjourned the meeting.

The chairman of Murphy Oil Corp. will retire next year.

**23.21** | Capitalize the pronoun "I" and its various contractions:

I have two cats and no dogs.

I'd love to go on vacation!

You and I have things to talk about.

I've lost my car keys.

I'll learn grammar eventually...I'm determined!

**23.22** | Capitalize all assumed names and names given for distinction.

| | |
|---|---|
| Attila the Hun | John Doe |
| Vlad the Impaler | John the Baptist |
| Alexander the Great | Spartacus |

**23.23** | Capitalize words that refer to significant events or periods in human history.

| | |
|---|---|
| Industrial Revolution | Civil War |
| Middle Ages | Stone Age |
| The Great Flood | Magna Carta |
| Vietnam War | Ice Age |

## Relative (Family) Words

**23.30** | When relative (or family) words such as *mother, father, brother, sister,* and *uncle* are used as common nouns, do not capitalize these words; but see the Rules 14.31, 14.32, and 14.33 for exceptions.

Julia's father would not let her go to the movie.

My mother was arrested for drunk driving; now she is in jail.

My brother and I bought new laptop computers.

I could not remember my aunt's last name!

**23.31** | When a relative word is used with a person's name, capitalize the word. But see Rule 23.32 for an exception involving possessive pronouns.

I called Uncle Joe to ask for a loan, but he said no.

I have not seen Aunt Emma for years.

My mother says Grandpa George is filthy rich.

**23.32** | When a relative word is preceded by a possessive pronoun (*my, her, his, your, their*), it is a common noun; write it in lowercase, even if it is used with a person's name. This rule conforms to Chicago Style; rules may vary in other writing style guides.

> I called my uncle Joe to ask for a loan, but he said no.

> I have not seen her aunt Emma for years.

> My father Jake is a carpenter by profession.

> I saw his brother Arthur at the grocery store.

**23.33** | Capitalize relative words written in place of a person's name.

> You might not agree, but Father knows best.

> Her father Jake works hard to earn a living.

> Did you buy a present for your mother?

> Yes, I bought these videos for Mother.

✱ TIP: If you can replace the relative word in a sentence with the person's name and the sentence still reads correctly, the relative word is a proper noun— capitalize it. As an example, let's use the name *Ruth* and the sentence *Did you buy a present for your mother?*

> Did you buy a present for *Mother*?

> Did you buy a present for *Ruth*?

☑ *Mother* can be replaced with *Ruth* and the sentence reads correctly; so here, the relative word "mother" is a proper noun and should be capitalized.

> Did you buy a present for your *mother*?

> Did you buy a present for your *Ruth*?

☑ Switching *mother* and *Ruth* in this sentence doesn't work, so the relative word "mother" is a common noun and not capitalized.

## Religious Titles and Terms

**23.40** | Pronouns that refer to the Supreme Being should be lowercased, according to Chicago Style. However, the CMoS Q&A website states that some religious writers and readers may be offended by this practice. The best approach is for writers to follow "house rules" of the publisher, or consider their intended audience and write pronouns that refer to the Supreme Being in uppercase or lowercase as appropriate.

The miracle of life is His work.

I trust that He will guide me.

**23.41** | Capitalize the names that refer to Christ.

Jesus Christ, Son of God, Man of Galilee, The Crucified, The Anointed One, Savior

**23.42** | Capitalize the names of God in all religions.

Christianity: God, Lord, Creator, Providence, Almighty, Heavenly Father, Holy One, God the Father

Judaism: Jehova, Yahweh, Adonai, YHWH, EL, Elohim, Eloah, El Shaddai, Tzevaot, Sabaoth

Islam: Allah; the 99 Names of God—Ar Rahman (The All Merciful);Al Malik (The King, The Sovereign); Al Quddus, and others

Hinduism: Brahma, Vishnu, Shiva, Rama, Krishna, Ganapati, Lakshmi, Indra, Surya, Agni, Durga Devi, Saraswati, and others.

**23.43** | Do not capitalize nonspecific uses of the word "god."

Zeus was the god of the sky and thunder in ancient Greece.

The king of the gods, Zeus, ruled the earth from Mount Olympus.

In Katmandu, Nepal, a group of young girls are worshipped as goddesses.

**23.44** | Capitalize the names of specific deities, and religious figures.

|  |  |  |
|---|---|---|
| Virgin Mary | Greek gods | Shiva |
| Moses | Muhammad | Buddha |
| Zeus | Poseidon | gods of Rome |

**23.45** | Capitalize the various names of God's evil detractor.

Beelzebub, Prince of Darkness, Satan, King of Hell, Devil, Tempter of Men, Father of Lies, Dark Lord, Evil One

**23.46** | Capitalize the names and designations of characters in the Bible and in the scriptures of other religions.

Lily of Israel, Rose of Sharon, Comfortress of the Afflicted, Help of Christians, Prince of the Apostles, Star of the Sea, John the Baptist

**23.47** | Capitalize proper nouns that refer to the Bible or scriptures of other religions, and to any particular parts of those texts.

Christianity: Holy Writ, Sacred Book, Holy Book, God's Word, Old Testament, New Testament, Gospel of St. Matthew.

Judaism: Hebrew Bible, Tanakh, Torah, Nevi'im, Ketuvim

Hinduism: Shruti, Vedas, Riveda, Aranyakas, Brahmanas, Upanishads, Bhagavad Gita, Ramayana, Panchatantra

Buddhism: Dhammapada, Tripitaka

Taoism: Tao Te Ching, Chuang Tzu, I Ching

Confucianism: The Analects of Confucius, I Ching

Islam: The Qur'an, Hadith, Sunnah

## Political Titles and Terms

**23.60** | Capitalize the names of cities, states, and provinces, but do not capitalize common nouns that refer to them, such as the word "city" in the phrase "city of Denver."

> I live in the city of Denver.
>
> He moved to the state of California.
>
> Vancouver is in the province of British Columbia.
>
> Ontario is one of the Canadian provinces.

**23.62** | Capitalize the titles of honorable, state, and political offices when used as part of a formal title. Otherwise, write these titles as common nouns in lowercase.

> President Barack Obama toured the school.
>
> Barack Obama was elected president of the United States in 2008.
>
> The company's top executive is Chairman Mark Murphy.
>
> Mark Murphy is chairman of the company.

**23.61** | Capitalize political titles and other official titles that directly precede names, but not the titles and designations that follow names.

> Carolyn worked as the assistant to Mayor Thompson.
>
> I was able to interview Gerald Thompson, mayor of Boston.

**23.63** | Capitalize the names of military organizations, bases, etc.

| | |
|---|---|
| U.S. Army | 3rd Regiment |
| the Army | the Navy |
| U.S. Navy | French Army |
| British Navy | Marine Corps |
| the Marines | the Air Force |
| U.S. Air Force | Royal Air Force |

**23.64** | Capitalize acronyms formed from the initials of organizations, well-known treaties, and countries.

| | | |
|---|---|---|
| FBI | CIA | USA |
| UN | NSA | EU |
| UNESCO | NATO | NAFTA |

**23.65** | Capitalize most acronyms formed from the first letters of several words, such as FYI, FAQ, and ASAP written in running text and dialogue. However, acronyms are commonly used in Internet discussion, chat, and mobile texting; when used in these contexts, they may be written uppercase or lowercase.

## Educational Titles and Terms

**23.80** | Capitalize the names of colleges and universities. But the terms "university" and "college" when used alone generally are common nouns and should not be capitalized.

Harvard University

College of the Canyons

The university student flunked his grammar exam.

Ask the college bookstore to stock this book.

**23.81** | Do not capitalize the words freshman, sophomore, junior, senior, or first-year student unless used at the beginning of a sentence or in a headline. When referring to students, upper-division is preferred to upper-class, and first-year is preferred to freshman.

**23.82** | Capitalize the names of college and university departments, and official bodies of educational organizations.

The School of Law is sometimes called the law school.

The Board of Regents decided to raise the tuition next year.

The School of Education grants teaching degrees to graduates.

I attended the University of California at Northridge.

When I attended the university, I took courses on art and science.

**23.83** | Capitalize letter grades earned in courses.

That girl should receive an A for effort.

He was given an F in math because he failed the final exam.

Betty has a C average in her classes; she can and should do better.

**23.84** | Write academic degrees in lowercase when used generically.

She received a law degree from Harvard University.

Allan is pursuing a bachelor's degree at Yale.

You must have a master's degree to apply for this job.

He earned a doctorate from Stanford University.

**23.85** | Capitalize educational degrees only when they directly precede or follow a person's name; otherwise, use lowercase (Chicago Style); or capitalize all degree names no matter where they appear (AP Style).

Chicago Manual of Style:

Elizabeth earned a master of science degree from Harvard.

Allan is pursuing a bachelor of education degree at Yale.

You must have a bachelor in computer science for this job.

*but...*

Bachelor of Education Allan Jones will speak at the seminar.

He introduced Johnathan Adams, Master of Journalism.

AP Style:

Elizabeth earned a Master of Science degree from Harvard University.

Allan is pursuing a Bachelor of Education degree at Yale.

You need a Bachelor in Computer Science for this job.

*and...*

Bachelor of Education Allan Jones will speak at the seminar.

He introduced Johnathan Adams, Master of Journalism.

**23.86** | Academic degree abbreviations require capitalization. The rules vary from one style guide to another. A few examples from Chicago Style and AP Style are shown below.

| Chicago | AP Style |
| --- | --- |
| PhD | Ph.D. |
| MA | M.A. |
| MS | M.S. |
| BS | B.S. |
| AA | A.A. |
| MBA | MBA |

## Job Titles

**23.90** | The rules for capitalizing job titles can be confusing. Generally, use lowercase for titles when preceded by an article (*a/an* or *the*); and for all titles used as common nouns.

Mr. Carlson is the editorial director for the Los Angeles Times.

Mr. Carlson, Editorial Director of the Los Angeles Times, spoke at the luncheon.

Bill Gates is the chairman of Microsoft Corp.

Bill Gates, Chairman of Microsoft Corp., previewed the new Windows 99 software.

Mr. Adams was the director of Media Blast Group.

Mr. Adams, Director of Media Blast Group, will retire soon.

**23.91** | When a person has an unusually long title, write the title after the name and in lowercase to avoid excessive capitalization that would look odd and be difficult to read.

Special Assistant to the Director of Special Campus Projects Allan West will be given additional job responsibilities when the fall semester begins.

☑️  The job title in the foregoing example contains numerous capital letters, and the sentence construction is awkward.

Allan West, special assistant to the director of special campus projects, will be given additional job responsibilities when the fall semester begins.

☑️  Placing a long title after a person's name, set off by commas, and writing it in lowercase is easier on the eyes and flows better.

**23.92** | Do not capitalize generic occupational descriptions, regardless of whether they precede or follow the person's name.

When writer Steven Clark met with publisher Elaine Sanders, they decided to launch a new publishing imprint devoted to cook books, led by editor Joe Wilson.

**23.93** | When a job title is part of an address or headline, capitalize the title, even if it is written after the name.

Craig Carson, Director of Public Affairs
Dept. of Building and Safety
P.O. Box 123456
Los Angeles CA 90010

# Chapter 24
## Titles of Books, Artwork, etc.

Writing style guides vary on how to write and format titles of books, articles, movies, paintings, and other similar works. In this chapter, we will follow the rules outlined in *Chicago Manual of Style*. Basically, some titles should be italicized, others should be enclosed within quotation marks, and still others should be written as plain text. For example, song titles should be enclosed in quote marks, but the names of the bands that recorded the songs are written with no italics or quotation marks.

The following rules will help you to write titles correctly and consistently. Note that references to "plain text" mean that the type of title being discussed should not be italicized or enclosed in quote marks.

**24.01** | Capitalize the first word and last word of every title. Capitalize all nouns, pronouns, adjectives, verbs, adverbs, and subordinating conjunctions. Capitalize prepositions only if they are used adverbially or adjectivally. Lowercase articles (*a, an, the*), coordinating conjunctions, and the word "to" in an infinitive, such as *How to Play the Violin*.

> *The Lord of the Rings*, a book by J. R. R. Tolkien, and a movie
>
> *Apocalypse Orphan*, a science-fiction novel by Tim Allen
>
> *The Creation of Adam*, a masterpiece by Michelangelo
>
> "Crazy in Love," a song performed by Beyoncé

**24.02** | Italicize titles of books, newspapers, and magazines. Italicize the word "The" only if it is formally part of the title.

> *You Can Change Your Life* is an inspiring, self-help book.

> Do you subscribe to *The New York Times*?

> *National Geographic* magazine features many color photographs.

**24.03** | Do not italicize widely known books such as The Bible, The Koran, and The Iliad.

> Mary reads The Bible, and Ahmed reads The Koran, but Jack prefers to read *The Los Angeles Times*.

**24.04** | Titles of book chapters and articles published in newspapers, magazines, and on websites should be enclosed in quotation marks.

> "Fatal Police Shooting Captured on Video" (*NBCNews.com*)

> "MacBook Air Will Never Likely Get an Update" (*Mashable.com*)

> "No Raise, No Title—Is It Still Considered a Promotion?" (*Forbes*)

> "Plan to Cut Medicare Drug Payments Raises Skepticism" (*The New York Times*)

**24.05** | Titles of journals, reports, studies, pamphlets, and handbooks should be italicized. But enclose essay titles in quotation marks.

> *New England Journal of Medicine*

> *Guide to Medical Records Privacy*

> *British Journal of Medicine*

> *Google Handbook for New-Hires*

> "Understanding the Criminal Mind" (Psych 101 Essay)

**24.06** | Website names should be treated as proper nouns and written in plain text with no italics or quote marks. Webpage titles and sections, however, should be enclosed in quotation marks.

Facebook

"Facebook Terms and Policies" (webpage title)

The Huffington Post

YouTube

Spectrum Ink Publishing

"Spectrum Ink Publishing FAQ" (web page title)

**24.07** | Italicize the names of blogs, including video blogs. But blog entries should be non-italicized and enclosed in quotation marks.

Blogs:

*TechCrunch*

*PerezHilton*

*Writing Life Blog*

Blog Entries:

"How Biometrics Are Changing Mobile Payments"

"Pokémon Go Is Launching on iOS and Android Today"

"Mötley Crüe Singer Vince Neil Charged with Assaulting Fan"

**24.08** | Titles of federal, state, county, and municipal legal statutes are italicized.

*United States Code*

*Title 21—Food and Drugs*

*Article I—Declaration of Rights (California)*

*Affordable Care Act*

**24.09** | Titles of movies and television programs should be italicized, but titles of television series episodes should be enclosed in quote marks.

*Mad Max: Fury Road*

*The Shawshank Redemption*

*Breaking Bad*

*X-Files*

*Game of Thrones*

"My Struggle" (X-Files episode)

"Home Again" (X-Files episode)

**24.10** | The titles of large or well-known fairs and exhibitions should be written as plain text, but small or lesser-known fairs and exhibitions should be italicized.

**24.11** | Titles of major software products should be treated as proper nouns and written as plain text. Titles of apps should be italicized.

Windows 10

Microsoft Office

Avast Antivirus

*Trello (app)*

*BrightNest (app)*

*Moodnotes (app)*

**24.12** | Titles of speeches and lecture series should be handled as proper nouns and written as plain text. Individual lectures within a series should be set off by quote marks.

Speeches:

I Have a Dream, a speech by Martin Luther King Jr.

The Great Silent Majority, a speech by Richard Nixon

Every Man a King, a speech by Huey Pierce Long

Lecture Series:

>The Charles Eliot Norton Lectures at Harvard University
>
>Distinctive Voices, by the National Academy of Sciences

Individual Lectures:

>"The Romantic Imagination" (C. M. Bowra, Charles Eliot Norton Lectures)
>
>"Tragedy in the Art of Music" (Leo Schrade, Charles Eliot Norton Lectures)

**24.13** | The correct way to handle music-related titles can be confusing. The approach outlined in *Chicago Manual of Style* requires using italics as well as quotation marks, depending on the nature of the title, as explained here:

• Song titles should be enclosed in quotation marks:

>"This Is What You Came For" by Calvin Harris
>
>"Dangerous Woman" by Ariana Grande
>
>"Needed Me" by Rihanna
>
>Prince wrote Chaka Khan's hit song, "I Feel for You,"

• Musical band names are written as proper nouns in plain text:

>Rolling Stones
>
>Metallica
>
>Coldplay
>
>Twenty One Pilots

• Album and CD titles should be italicized:

>*Lemonade* by Beyonce
>
>*True Sadness* by The Avett Brothers
>
>*The Getaway* by Red Hot Chili Peppers

- Classical music titles should be written in plain text:

  Symphony No. 5 in C Minor by Ludwig van Beethoven

  The Valkyrie: Ride of the Valkyries by Richard Wagner

  Adagio for Strings, composed by Samuel Barber

- Opera titles should be italicized:

  *The Marriage of Figaro,* composed by Wolfgang Amadeus Mozart

  *Der Ring des Nibelungen,* composed by Richard Wagner

  *Madame Butterfly,* composed by Giacomo Puccini

**24.14** | Italicize titles of artwork, paintings, drawings, and photographs.

  *Mona Lisa* by Leonardo da Vinci

  *The Creation of Adam* by Michelangelo

  *Starry Night* by Vincent van Gogh

**24.15** | Italicize titles of radio programs and podcasts. But enclose episodes of podcasts and radio programs in quotation marks.

  *Morning Edition*

  *All Things Considered*

  *Fresh Air*

  *The Kim Komando Show*

  "From 'Runt of the Litter' to Liberal Icon: The Story of Robert Kennedy" (episode of *Fresh Air*)

**24.16** | Titles of cartoons and comic strips should be italicized.

  *Dilbert*

  *Garfield*

*The Far Side*

*Superman*

*Hagar the Horrible*

**24.17** | Titles of plays should be italicized.

*Death of A Salesman* (1949) by Arthur Miller

*A Streetcar Named Desire* (1947) by Tennessee Williams

*Who's Afraid of Virginia Woolf?* (1962) by Edward Albee

*Long Day's Journey into Night* (1956) by Eugene O'Neill

**24.18** | Poem titles should be enclosed in quotation marks, unless the poem is book-length, and then it should be italicized. Books and anthologies of poetry should be handled in the same manner as other books (italicized).

"Phenomenal Woman" by Maya Angelou

"The Road Not Taken" by Robert Frost

"A Dream Within a Dream" by Edgar Allan Poe

**24.19** | Short story titles should be enclosed in quotation marks. An anthology or book-length collection of short stories is handled as a typical book and the title is italicized, but the titles of individual short stories in the book are enclosed in quotation marks.

"The Gift of the Magi" by O. Henry

"The Little Match Girl" by Hans Christian Andersen

"To Build a Fire" by Jack London

*Great Short Stories of the Masters* (anthology)

*The Best American Short Stories of the Century* (anthology)

**24.20** | Enclose the titles of unpublished books in quotation marks. An unpublished work that would be written in italics if it were published as described in this chapter also should be enclosed in quotation marks.

"The Incredible Journey to Mars" (unpublished sci-fi novel)

"Little Red and the Stalker" (unpublished short story)

"I Dream of Tomorrow" (unpublished poem)

**24.21** | Ship and vessel names should be italicized, including ships on water, in space, and in the air.

| | |
|---|---|
| USS *Constitution* | HMS *Victory* |
| Shuttle *Endeavor* | RMS *Titanic* |
| *Hindenburg* | The *Santa Maria* |
| *Spruce Goose* | NASA's *Juno* probe |

Do not italicize abbreviations for United States Ship (USS), Her Majesty's Ship (HMS), Royal Mail Ship (RMS), and similar identifying prefixes.

# Conclusion

This concludes our brief primer on grammar, style, and punctuation. I hope you found this style guide easy to read and that it will help move your writing to the next level in the weeks ahead.

**Please post a review!** If you enjoyed this book, please take just a minute or two to visit your favorite online bookseller and post a review. Any feedback you share will be appreciated and will help spread the word about this book to others. Thank you!

**Network with Other Writers!** If you enjoy networking with writers and other creative people, join SPECTRUM, a social network for writers and other talented creators. Connect with editors, reviewers, cover designers, beta readers, and build your fan following in a fun and creative environment. Visit http://my.vu.org/ today.

# Appendix A
## Internet Acronyms

| | |
|---|---|
| *G* | giggle or grin |
| *H* | hug |
| *K* | kiss |
| *S* | smile |
| *T* | tickle |
| *W* | wink |
| 2MFM | too much for me |
| 2U2 | to you too |
| 404 | dead link |
| 4AYN | for all you know |
| 4SALE | for sale |
| 4U | for you |
| =w= | whatever |
| >U | screw you |
| ? | huh? |
| Q4U | question for you |
| A/S/L | age/sex/location |
| AAMOF | as a matter of fact |
| ABT | about |
| AND | any day now |
| AFAIC | as far as I'm concerned |

| | |
|---|---|
| AFAICS | as far as I can see |
| AFAICT | as far as I can tell |
| AFAIK | as far as I know |
| AFAYC | as far as you're concerned |
| AFK | away from keyboard |
| AISI | as I see it |
| AIUI | as I understand it |
| AKA | also known as |
| AML | all my love |
| ASAP | as soon as possible |
| ASL | age, sex, location |
| ASLP | age, sex, location, picture |
| ATM | at this moment |
| AWA | as well as |
| AWOL | away without leave |
| AYOR | at your own risk |
| AYPI? | and your point is? |
| B/C | because |
| B4 | before |
| BAC | back at the computer |
| BAK | back at the keyboard |
| BBL | be back later |
| BBS | be back soon |
| BBS | bulletin board system |
| BC | be cool |

| | |
|---|---|
| BCnU | be seeing you |
| BF | boyfriend |
| BFN | bye for now |
| BG | big grin |
| BION | believe it or not |
| BITM | but in the meantime |
| BKA | better known as |
| BM | bite me |
| BOL | be on later |
| BOT | back on topic |
| BRB | be right back |
| BRBS | be right back soon |
| BRH | be right here |
| BS | bullsh*t |
| BSF | but seriously folks |
| BST | but seriously though |
| BTA | but then again |
| BTAIM | be that as it may |
| BTDT | been there done that |
| BTSOOM | beats the sh*t out of me |
| BTW | by the way |
| BYOB | bring your own bottle |
| CAD | ctrl-alt-delete |
| CDIWY | couldn't do it without you |
| CFY | calling for you |

| | |
|---|---|
| CID | crying in disgrace |
| CLM | career limiting move |
| CM@TW | catch me at the Web |
| CMIIW | correct me if I'm wrong |
| CNP | continue in next post |
| CRS | can't remember sh*t |
| CTS | changing the subject |
| CU | see you |
| CU2 | see you too |
| CUL | see you later |
| CUL8R | see you later |
| CWOT | complete waste of time |
| CWYL | chat with you later |
| CYA | cover your ass |
| DBA | doing business as |
| DCed | disconnected |
| DH | dear husband |
| DIIK | damned if I know |
| DIKU | do I know you? |
| DIRTFT | do it right the first time |
| DIY | do it yourself |
| DL | download |
| DND | do not disturb |
| DQMOT | don't quote me on this |
| DTC | damn this computer |

| | |
|---|---|
| DTRT | do the right thing |
| DUCT | did you see that? |
| DW | dear wife |
| DWAI | don't worry about it |
| DYK | do you know |
| EAK | eating at keyboard |
| EMFBI | excuse me for butting in |
| EMFJI | excuse me for jumping in |
| EOD | end of discussion |
| EOF | end of file |
| EOL | end of lecture |
| EOM | end of message |
| EOS | end of story |
| EOT | end of thread |
| F | female |
| F2F | face to face |
| FAQ | frequently asked questions |
| FAWC | for anyone who cares |
| FB | Facebook |
| FBOW | for better or worse |
| FBTW | fine, be that way |
| FCOL | for crying out loud |
| FIFO | first in, first out |
| FISH | first in, still here |
| FOAD | f**k off and die |

| | |
|---|---|
| FOAF | friend of a friend |
| FOC | free of charge |
| FOS | freedom of speech |
| FTTT | from time to time |
| FU | f**ked up |
| FUBAR | f**ked up beyond all recognition |
| FWIW | for what it's worth |
| FYA | for your amusement |
| FYE | for your entertainment |
| FYEO | for your eyes only |
| FYI | for your information |
| G | grin |
| G2B | going to bed |
| G2G | got to go |
| GA | good afternoon |
| GAFIA | get away from it all |
| GAL | get a life |
| GBH | great big hug |
| GD&H | grinning, ducking and hiding |
| GD&R | grinning, ducking and running |
| GD&W | grin, duck and wave |
| GDW | grin, duck and wave |
| GE | good evening |
| GF | girlfriend |
| GFETE | grinning from ear to ear |

| | |
|---|---|
| GFN | gone for now |
| GFU | good for you |
| GG | good game |
| GGU2 | good game, you two |
| GIGO | garbage in garbage out |
| GJ | good job |
| GL | good luck |
| GM | good morning, or good match |
| GMAB | give me a break |
| GMAO | giggling my ass off |
| GMBO | giggling my butt off |
| GMTA | great minds think alike |
| GN | good night |
| GOK | god only knows |
| GOWI | get on with it |
| GR8 | great |
| GtG | got to go |
| GTSY | glad to see you |
| H&K | hug and kiss |
| H/O | hold on |
| HAG1 | have a good one |
| HAGD | have a good day |
| HAGN | have a good night |
| HB | hug back |
| HB | hurry back |

| | |
|---|---|
| HHIS | hanging head in shame |
| HHJK | ha ha, just kidding |
| HHOJ | ha ha, only joking |
| HHOK | ha ha, only kidding |
| HHOS | ha ha, only seriously |
| HIH | hope it helps |
| HLM | he loves me |
| HMS | hanging my self |
| HMWK | homework |
| HOAS | hold on a second |
| HSIK | how should I know |
| HTH | hope this helps |
| IAC | in any case |
| IAE | in any event |
| IAG | it's all good |
| IC | I see |
| IDC | I don't care |
| IDGI | I don't get it |
| IDGW | in a good way |
| IDI | I doubt it |
| IDK | I don't know |
| IDTT | I'll drink to that |
| IFVB | I feel very bad |
| IGP | I gotta pee |
| IGTP | I get the point |

| | |
|---|---|
| IHU | I hate you |
| IHY | I hate you |
| II | I'm impressed |
| IIR | if I recall |
| IIRC | if I recall correctly |
| IIT | I'm impressed too |
| IJWTK | I just want to know |
| IJWTS | I just want to say |
| IK | I know |
| IKWUM | I know what you mean |
| ILU | I love you |
| ILY | I love you |
| ILYFAE | I love you forever and ever |
| IME | in my experience |
| IMHO | in my humble opinion |
| IMNSHO | in my not-so-humble opinion |
| IMO | in my opinion |
| IMP | I might be pregnant |
| INPO | in no particular order |
| IOW | in other words |
| IRL | in real life |
| IRMFI | I reply merely for information |
| IS | I'm sorry |
| ISTM | it seems to me |
| ISTR | I seem to recall |

| | |
|---|---|
| ISWYM | I see what you mean |
| ITFA | in the final analysis |
| ITRW | in the real world |
| ITSFWI | if the shoe fits, wear it |
| IVL | in virtual life |
| IYKWIM | if you know what I mean |
| IYSWIM | if you see what I mean |
| J/K | just kidding |
| J/P | just playing |
| JAM | just a minute |
| JAS | just a second |
| JIC | just in case |
| JJWY | just joking with you |
| JK | just kidding |
| JMHO | just my humble opinion |
| JMO | just my opinion |
| JP | just playing |
| JTLYK | just to let you know |
| JW | just wondering |
| K | okay |
| KB | kiss back |
| KHYF | know how you feel |
| KISS | keep it simple stupid |
| KIT | keep in touch |
| KMA | kiss my ass |

| | |
|---|---|
| KMB | kiss my butt |
| KOTC | kiss on the cheek |
| KOTL | kiss on the lips |
| KUTGW | keep up the good work |
| KWIM | know what I mean? |
| L8R | later |
| LAB | life's a bitch |
| LAM | leave a message |
| LD | long distance |
| LG | lovely greetings |
| LHM | Lord help me |
| LHU | Lord help us |
| LIMH | laughing in my head |
| LMA | leave me alone |
| LMAO | laughing my ass off |
| LMBO | laughing my butt off |
| LMFAO | laughing my fat ass off |
| LMHO | laughing my head off |
| LMK | let me know |
| LOL | laughing out loud |
| LOLA | laughing out loud again |
| LOML | light of my life (or love of my life) |
| LOOL | laughing out outrageously loud |
| LSHIPMP | laughing so hard I peed my pants |
| LTNS | long time no see |

| | |
|---|---|
| LTR | long term relationship |
| LTS | laughing to self |
| LULAS | love you like a sister |
| LYK | let you know |
| LYL | love ya lots |
| M | male |
| M8 | mate |
| MB | maybe |
| MYOB | mind your own business |
| N/C | not cool |
| N/M | never mind / nothing much |
| N/S | no shit |
| N2M | not too much |
| NE1 | Anyone |
| NFI | no freaking idea |
| NL | not likely |
| NM | never mind / nothing much |
| NMH | not much here |
| NMJC | nothing much, just chillin' |
| NOM | no offense meant |
| NOYB | none of your business |
| NOYFB | none of your freaking business |
| NP | no problem |
| NVM | never mind |
| OBTW | oh, by the way |

| | |
|---|---|
| OFIS | on floor with stitches |
| OIC | oh, I see |
| OL | old lady (wife, girlfriend) |
| OM | old man (husband, boyfriend) |
| OMG | oh my God / gosh / goodness |
| OOC | out of character |
| OT | off-topic |
| OTOH | on the other hand |
| OTTOMH | off the top of my head |
| P@H | parents at home |
| PAH | parents at home |
| PAW | parents are watching |
| PITA | pain in the ass |
| PLZ | please |
| PM | private message |
| PMFJI | pardon me for jumping in |
| PMJI | pardon my jumping in (variation of PMFJI) |
| PMP | peed my pants |
| POAHF | put on a happy face |
| POOF | I have left the chat |
| POS | parents over shoulder |
| POTB | pats on the back |
| PPL | people |
| PS | post script |
| PSA | public show of affection |

| | |
|---|---|
| Q4U | question for you |
| QT | cutie |
| RME | rolling my eyes |
| ROFL | rolling on floor laughing |
| ROFLMAO | rolling on floor laughing my ass off |
| ROFLOL | rolling on floor laughing out loud |
| ROTFL | rolling on the floor laughing |
| RTF | read the FAQ |
| RTFM | read the freaking manual |
| RTSM | read the stupid manual |
| RUTTM | are you talking to me |
| RVD | really very dumb |
| S/U | shut up |
| SH | same here |
| SH | so hot |
| SHID | slaps head in disgust |
| SNAFU | situation normal, all fouled up |
| SO | significant other |
| SOHF | sense of humor failure |
| SOMY | sick of me yet? |
| SPAM | stupid person's advertisement |
| SRY | sorry |
| SSDD | same sh*t different day |
| STBY | sucks to be you |
| STFU | shut the f**k up |

| | |
|---|---|
| STI | stick(ing) to it |
| STW | search the web |
| SWAK | sealed with a kiss |
| SWB | sorry, wrong box |
| SWL | screaming with laughter |
| SYS | see you soon |
| SYSOP | system operator |
| TA | thanks again |
| TCO | taken care of |
| TGIF | thank God it's Friday |
| THTH | too hot to handle |
| THX | thanks |
| TIA | thanks in advance |
| TJM | that's just me |
| TMA | take my advice |
| TMI | too much information |
| TOH | the other half |
| TOY | thinking of you |
| TPTB | the powers that be |
| TSDMC | tears streaming down my cheeks |
| TT2T | too tired to talk |
| TTFN | ta ta for now |
| TTT | thought that, too |
| TTUL | talk to you later |
| TTYIAM | talk to you in a minute |

| | |
|---|---|
| TTYL | talk to you later |
| TTYLMF | talk to you later my friend |
| TTYS | talk to you soon |
| TU | thank you |
| TWMA | till we meet again |
| TX | thanks |
| TY | thank you |
| TYVM | thank you very much |
| U2 | you too |
| UAPITA | you're a pain in the ass |
| UR | your |
| UW | you're welcome |
| VBG | very big grin |
| VBS | very big smile |
| W/E | whatever |
| W8 | wait |
| WAY | who are you |
| WB | welcome back |
| WBS | write back soon |
| WE | whatever |
| WFM | works for me |
| WP | wrong person |
| WTF | what the f**k? |
| WTG | way to go |
| WTGP | want to go private? |

| | |
|---|---|
| WTH | what the heck? |
| WTMI | way too much information |
| WU | what's up? |
| WUF | where are you from? |
| WUWT | what's up with that? |
| WYMM | will you marry me? |
| WYSIWYG | what you see is what you get |
| Y | Why? |
| Y2K | you're too kind |
| YATB | you are the best |
| YBS | you'll be sorry |
| YG | young gentleman |
| YL | you'll live |
| YM | you mean |
| YMMD | you've made my day |
| YMMV | your mileage may vary |
| YOYO | you're on your own |
| YVM | you're very welcome |
| YW | you're welcome |
| YWIA | you're welcome in advance |
| YY4U | two wise for you |

# More Books from Spectrum Ink!

## As A Man Thinks

### Edited by Richard De A'Morelli

*(Inspirational/Self-Help)*

This special edition of James Allen's classic book *As a Man Thinketh* explores how the power of thought affects you on every level, and how you can take control of your life and destiny. The way you think creates every condition in your life, good and bad. If you have been beset by disappointment and failure, the empowering wisdom in this book can change your life. You will learn how to use the power of your mind to build confidence, unlock hidden talents, cope with depression and stress, overcome habits, and achieve health and vitality. Learn how to use these timeless insights to build a bright future and become the master of your destiny.

This edition retains the flavor of James Allen's practical advice but the book has been updated to a modern style that is easy to follow and enjoyable to read. Also, the book has been expanded—each chapter includes additional insights, explanations, and points to remember that can empower you to change your life by changing the way you think.

**Available online or visit:** http://spectrum.org/books/

| | |
|---|---|
| 978-1-988236-08-7 | MOBI/Kindle |
| 978-1-988236-09-4 | EPUB Digital |
| 978-1-988236-10-0 | Paperback |
| 978-1-988236-11-7 | Paperback Large Print |
| 978-1-988236-12-4 | Hardcover Edition |

# Apocalypse Orphan
## By Tim Allen

*(Science Fiction-Fantasy)*

Commander Orlando Iron Wolf is aboard the International Space Station when a blinking light on his computer console alerts him to a fast moving comet headed for a collision with planet Earth.

With no way to stop the impending doomsday, the world descends into panic and anarchy. Massive transport ships are built to colonize the moon, and evacuation of a chosen few begins.

After a shuttle mission to study the approaching comet goes awry, Wolf is forced into cryogenic deep sleep, and the onboard computer assumes control of the ship.

Wolf awakens 50,000 years later to a wildly different earth. Endowed with incredible strength, he finds himself caught in a war between primitive tribes, and his survival depends on Syn, an advanced computer intelligence who has fallen in love with him.

Will Wolf be able to help restore Earth to its past glory or is civilization doomed to fail?

**Available online or visit:** http://spectrum.org/books/

| ISBN Numbers | Editions |
|---|---|
| 978-1-988236-00-1 | MOBI/Kindle |
| 978-1-988236-07-0 | EPUB Digital |
| 978-1-988236-01-8 | Paperback |
| 978-1-088236-02-5 | Paperback Large Print |
| 978-1-988236-03-2 | Hardcover Edition |

# Live Well. Be Happy.
## by Richard De A'Morelli
*(Inspirational/Self-Help)*

This book is about your life and your search for happiness. It will help you to realize that you can change your life by changing how you think and react to the world around you. You will learn steps you can take to stay sane, positive, and balanced in a crazy world. And you will discover how making simple changes in your daily routine can help you find your path to happiness.

In these pages, you will learn that happiness in life depends on the choices you make, staying positive, and never giving up on your hopes and dreams. You'll discover simple methods to reduce stress, overcome depression, build confidence, and conquer unhealthy habits. You will also learn how to stay balanced and maintain your peace of mind using natural techniques such as visualization, rhythm breathing, and meditation.

This inspiring little book reminds us that life is short, and we must make the most of the precious time we are given. If you have been looking for a book that will encourage you to change your life and give you a helping hand to move forward, this short course in modern living may be that inspiration. The book also makes a wonderful gift for someone in need of encouragement and a step-by-step approach to getting their life on a positive track.

**Buy online or visit:** http://vu.org/books/live-well/live-well

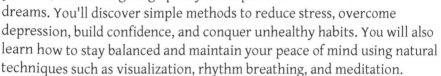

|  |  |
|---|---|
| 978-1-988234-09-3 | MOBI/Kindle |
| 978-1-988234-08-6 | EPUB Digital |
| 978-1-988234-04-8 | Paperback |
| 978-1-988234-04-9 | Paperback Large Print |
| 978-1-988236-46-9 | Paperback (retail) |

Made in the
USA
Monee, IL